Fundraising and
Strategic Planning

Innovative Approaches
for Museums

About the Series

The *Innovative Approaches for Museums* series offers case studies, written by scholars and practitioners from museums, galleries, and other institutions, that showcase the original, transformative, and sometimes wholly re-invented methods, techniques, systems, theories, and actions that demonstrate innovative work being done in the museum and cultural sector throughout the world. The authors come from a variety of institutions—in size, type, budget, audience, mission, and collection scope. Each volume offers ideas and support to those working in museums while serving as a resource and primer, as much as inspiration, for students and the museum staff and faculty training future professionals who will further develop future innovative approaches.

About the Series Editor

Juilee Decker is an associate professor of Museum Studies at Rochester Institute of Technology (RIT) where she teaches courses focusing on museums and technology so as to bring theory and praxis together in the classroom environment. She has worked as a public art consultant and advisor for more than 15 years and has managed several public and private collections of public art. Since 2008, she has served as editor of *Collections: A Journal for Museum and Archives Professionals*, a peer-reviewed journal published by Rowman & Littlefield.

Fundraising and Strategic Planning

Innovative Approaches for Museums

Edited by Juilee Decker

ROWMAN & LITTLEFIELD
Lanham • Boulder • New York • London

Published by Rowman & Littlefield
A wholly owned subsidiary of The Rowman & Littlefield Publishing Group, Inc.
4501 Forbes Boulevard, Suite 200, Lanham, Maryland 20706
www.rowman.com

Unit A, Whitacre Mews, 26-34 Stannary Street, London SE11 4AB

British Library Cataloguing in Publication Information Available

Library of Congress Cataloging-in-Publication Data
Fundraising and strategic planning : innovative approaches for museums /
edited by Juilee Decker.
    pages cm. — (Innovative approaches for museums)
  Includes bibliographical references and index.
  ISBN 978-1-4422-3877-0 (paperback : alkaline paper) — ISBN 978-1-4422-3878-
7 (electronic) 1. Museum finance. 2. Fund raising. 3. Museums—Marketing.
4. Public-private sector cooperation. 5. Museum visitors—Economic aspects. 6.
Crowd funding. 7. Museums—Management. 8. Strategic planning. I. Decker,
Juilee. II. Title: Fund raising and strategic planning.
  AM122.F87 2015
  069.068'1—dc23
                                                                2015011697

∞™ The paper used in this publication meets the minimum requirements of
American National Standard for Information Sciences—Permanence of Paper
for Printed Library Materials, ANSI / NISO Z39.48-1992.

Printed in the United States of America

Contents

Introduction

Fundraising and strategic planning are inextricably linked. Charitable dollars impact museums every single day across the United States and abroad by keeping doors open, underwriting programming and membership costs, and sustaining collections. Such monies allow for the achievement of objectives and performance targets in support of the institutional mission, values, and vision. Evidence of support may be gleaned from a search of informational tax forms filed by museums, including Internal Revenue Service (IRS) Form 990. A more exciting—and certainly more discursive—means of visualizing support comes from media coverage.

Over the past year, museums and their visitors have benefitted tremendously from grant-funded initiatives that aimed to connect visitors with the collections they love. One instance is a suite of projects underwritten by billionaire philanthropist and former mayor of New York, Michael Bloomberg, that proffers the use of digital technologies as key engagement pieces in the onsite museum experience in four U.S. museums as well as one in London and another in Singapore. The projects focus on immersive experiences that engage and further connect visitors with a single work or several from a collection. Apropos of its context, an interactive pen has become the tool of choice for visitors to the design museum—Cooper Hewitt Smithsonian Design Museum. This pen (or, due to its size and its capability, perhaps it should be *the Pen?*) enables visitors to add digital records of objects from the museum collection to the visitor's own portfolio of items. At the conclusion of one's visit, the Pen is given back to the museum and, in return, visitors may obtain information and images that they have captured. As Robinson Meyer reported in *The Atlantic*, this tool bridges the physical and the digital—a proposition that every gallery, library, archive, museum, and other collections-based organizations aims to achieve.[1]

1

The Pen and Cooper Hewitt model best practices in terms of what museums must do to thrive: they need to engage in authentic dialogue about their past, their present, and their future. Even if not called as such, they need to *reinvent* (or, even, *reaffirm* their present iteration) and to undertake *strategic planning* to bring their institutions to the next level however defined, conceived, and executed.[2] Through collaborative efforts, the Cooper Hewitt has brought design—its content—into the experience of the visitor through context entirely. For instance, the employ of the Pen (a design object extraordinaire) connects the visitor with the collections before them while capturing an account of the onsite experience. The Pen is supplemented by touch-screen tables that allow for collections view and an immersion room where The Pen becomes a tool of design for the user. The experience is both immersive and social all at once. So while this project, at its core, is a technological and digital innovation, the foundation, reach, and outcomes boast of the benefits achieved through fundraising and strategic planning.

Other projects benefitting from the aforementioned Bloomberg funds include an engaging, hands-on journey through the information age at the Science Museum, London, and an extension of the existing location-based and digital efforts of the American Museum of Natural History that updates their Explore app (launched in 2010) to version 2.0 to allow for personalized journeys and new ways to share experiences at the exhibits. The Brooklyn Museum will use funds to enable visitors to navigate through the galleries and to ask, through their mobile devices or museum-provided devices in stations through the museum, questions that will, in turn, be answered by staff in real time. Geo-positioning will enable staff to respond face-to-face to visitors in the galleries as well. The outcome of this three-year project will "create a dynamic and responsive museum that fosters dialogue and sparks conversation between staff and all Museum visitors."[3] In commenting upon the grant and the overall plan for the institution, the vice director of Digital Engagement and Technology at the Brooklyn Museum remarked that "the Museum has a community-driven mission and, in the past, we've often used technology to foster personal interaction in a way that treats each individual as unique and aims to give our visitors a sense of ownership in the institution. This project will do the same and such a significant grant allows us to do so on a scale that rethinks the entire museum experience from a visitor's entry to exit."[4] Bernstein's comments speak to the coherence of mission to practice that undergirds vibrant museums that seek to innovate.

Currently undergoing renovation and slated to reopen in 2016, the San Francisco Museum of Modern Art (SFMOMA) will marry the innovation and creativity that the Bay Area museum serves by offering a "fifth wall" in the galleries; that is, the museum's digital program will provide a space for experimentation.[5]

Established in 2012, Singapore's urban recreation space, Gardens by the Bay, will use Bloomberg funds to create an app that will integrate the natural world with the virtual by taking visitors on a journey through the Gardens with the aid of interactive trails and engaging activities.[6] As Michael Bloomberg noted, "Each of the institutions we're supporting is using technology in different ways to engage, educate, and immerse their visitors—and to make their world-class resources available to a greater number of people, more of the time."[7]

Fundraising and Strategic Planning: Innovative Approaches for Museums examines a range of ambitious undertakings and the means by which museums and cultural organizations achieve them. The foci in this volume are, truly, cornerstones to museum operations: strategic planning and fundraising. A strategic plan drives a museum's goals and activities and, on some level, the everyday. The plan is informed by a vision that describes what the museum will look like in the future. Both of these are informed by, and responsive to, fundraising (well, frankly, what in a museum *is not?*)

As with many of the topics in this series, the content areas in *Fundraising and Strategic Planning* overlap to some extent and are intentionally linked in this volume. In conceiving of this volume, I envisioned fundraising and strategic planning as ways of building bridges between the collections and people as well as connecting each of these groups of people— staff, visitors, donors, and other constituencies. Moreover, I consider each of these a flipside of a transparent coin. To explain, fundraising and strategic planning require transparency that, done well, cannot be minimized and rather *becomes* an expectation. As stewards of collections and fiduciary caretakers, museum professionals have a responsibility to be truthful about the institution's mission, intended use of funds, and capacity of the institution to use donations effectively for the intended purpose.

ABOUT THE INNOVATIVE APPROACHES FOR MUSEUMS SERIES

This series offers case studies, written by scholars and practitioners from museums, galleries, and other institutions, that showcase the original, transformative, and sometimes wholly reinvented methods, techniques, systems, theories, and actions that demonstrate innovative work being done in the museum and cultural sector throughout the United States and in England, Australia, and Peru. The authors come from a variety of institutions—in size, type, budget, audience, mission, and collection scope. Their geographical, authorial, and institutional diversity was an intentional part of crafting of this series as a means of offering a range of perspectives on issues confronting museums, and collecting institutions at large in some cases, that may be replicated entirely or scaled up or down by colleagues elsewhere.

Each chapter carefully examines a core issue by describing background information before turning to the identification of the problem, a solution to the issue, implementation, results, feedback, and assessment as well as next steps. Many chapters are enhanced with notes and/or resources to point the reader to contextual and additional information. Written with attention to the audience of peers and colleagues-in-training, each chapter is intended to offer ideas and support to those working in museums while serving as a resource and primer, as much as inspiration, for students and the museum staff and faculty training future professionals who will further develop future innovative approaches.

The volumes in this series are grouped under the following themes: technology and digital initiatives; engagement and access; collections care and stewardship; and fundraising and strategic planning. While each volume has a particular focus, the chapters in each volume rarely address the framing theme of that volume alone. Instead, the reach of the content often dapples in other aspects of that institution's operations. Such intersection and overlap speak to the integrative nature of museum work,[8] as museums function optimally when their areas of operation are not constrained to silos but, rather, when collaboration becomes the driver. An example of this "optimization for innovation," as I like to think of it, is the pioneering work done by the team at the Cleveland Museum of Art who, in their efforts to bring the museum into conversation with its audiences in multiple, meaningful ways and, ultimately, to become more visitor-centered. Their collaboration yielded Gallery One, an innovative space that fuses art, technology, and interpretation. This space in the museum has become a destination for visitors interested in learning more about art through a variety of hands-on interactives, including the forty-foot microtile multi-touch Collection Wall. Not content merely to implant digital technology and interactives in the gallery, this museum's refocusing on the visitor—as a recasting of the triangulation between the museum, its collections, and its viewers—required changes beyond those in the physical space of Gallery One, such as clearer pathways through the galleries and other new amenities that enmeshed the onsite visitor with an entirely new experience-based, interactive visit. Such optimization for innovation required a team of collaborators, who are cited prominently on the museum's website which notes that this project and the broader initiatives associated therein represent "a true and equal collaboration among the curatorial, information management and technology services, education and interpretation, and design departments at the Cleveland Museum of Art."[9] The chapter addressing this project appears in the volume on technology and digital initiatives, although the case study speaks to each of the other foci of the other three volumes in this series. Just as this project's design, implementation, and maintenance required the collaboration of a number of museum staff from many departments, so too may the case study, and all others in this series, find a home among many departments in your museum.

ABOUT THESE CASE STUDIES

Fundraising and Strategic Planning: Innovative Approaches for Museums appraises strategies museums employ to raise funds including admission prices, membership categories, donor and affinity groups, and specialized event-driven efforts while examining new crowdfunding models such as Kickstarter, Indiegogo, and Piggybackr. Consideration is also paid to the importance of thoughtful action and strategic planning as harbingers of success in many areas.

Specifically, crowdfunding and some measure of traditional fundraising are addressed in the case studies offered by Peter J. Kim of the Museum · of Food and Drink (New York, NY); Karen Gillenwater, formerly of Carnegie Center for Art and History (New Albany, IN); and Melissa A. Russo, Chabot Space and Science Center (Oakland, CA). These authors give practical advice as well as ruminations on process while offering thoughtful choices and intentionality concerning audience, reach, and inclusion.

This volume also pays heed to the importance of thoughtful action and strategic planning in yielding success in many areas of museum operations and sustainability. Mike Deetsch and Greg Hardison present the formulation and success of a pilot program at the Kentucky Historical Society. Launched in 2010, Camp ArtyFact was designed to solve a programming issue (which it did) and, since its iteration and continuous assessment and revision, has also created a shift in thinking about staffing and models of income. Nancy Enterline, Monterey Bay Aquarium, discusses how the institution leveraged market research to yield greater connection to the reasons why individuals commit to traditional membership models versus affinity groups. Karen Coutts addresses the needs of audiences and membership as outreach in her discussion of the program she initiated at The New Children's Museum entitled "Check It Out!" which put membership cards into circulation in public libraries. Coutts launched the program in 2008 and it still gains traction, as American Alliance of Museums members can attest, given the buzz on the list serve surrounding this topic in December 2014.

Fundraising and Strategic Planning also examines transparency, communication, and partnerships. Carl G. Hamm describes how the Saint Louis Art Museum moved from a capital campaign into a sustainable stream of increased annual giving. Vicky U. Lee narrates the transformation of abandoned, elevated rail yards into an exciting, well-traveled (and highly-tagged and pinned) public amenity, the High Line. While not a museum per se, the High Line and its public art amenities offer much to the story of collecting institutions, as well as to the framework of the public-private partnership. Jill Hartz, Jordan Schnitzer Museum of Art at the University of Oregon, shares her thirty-plus years of experience from academic museums to tell the importance of cultivating the administration, alumni, faculty and students, as well as the community. Colleagues in the Bay Area, James G. Leventhal and Irina Zeylikovich, provide development staff at all levels with advice on cultivating relevance, relationships, and resources. Rounding out the volume, Amy Gilman recounts the transformation of the Toledo Museum of Art (TMA) anchored in a strategic plan and restructuring (beautifully illustrating the symbiotic practice undertaken at TMA in the form of a butterfly diagram).

In addition to amazing generosity to propel the museum experience further, this past year saw the rescuing of a museum when U.S. foundations pledged hundreds of millions of dollars to rescue Detroit from bankruptcy and, in turn, to avoid liquidating its city-owned art collections at the Detroit Institute of Arts.[10] Collections matter and so do the spaces that house them. The space of the museum and its site are of primary importance, as evidenced by the Bloomberg projects addressed above which demonstate how grant-funded projects can serve to refocus our museums. Beyond those examples, several other key projects demonstrate the place of the museum, as opposed to its digital surrogate. For instance, the Indianapolis Museum of Art (IMA) gained support through a $1 million grant from the Efroymson Family Foundation that will support a new programming initiative called ARTx that aims to showcase the museum's role as a community center for the twenty-first century—an exploration station in our experience economy. The premise of ARTx is that events come in all shapes, sizes, and persuasions. Funded through 2018, ARTx programming will include: a mobile ARTx truck to take programming across the IMA campus and into the surrounding community; a musical performance and treat to one-of-a-kind menu from local chefs in a sensory experience called "Avant Brunch"; and a riff on the explosive (and controversial) exercise regiment, CrossFit, with ARTx Fit: Action in Art where attendees engage in an "intensive four-week immersion course" to "muscle up your art knowledge through discussions and making activities . . . [through the] address works from all eras of art."[11] Fundraising also furthers long-range, brick-and-mortar construction projects. Altria

Group gave $1 million to the National Museum of African America.. History and Culture as part of the capital campaign that will add an impressive 400,000-square-foot museum on the Mall and the nineteenth Smithsonian Institution.[12] Beyond these two examples, we can find many other instances where funding supports an institution's vision. In fact, it upholds it.

But, who are these donors, really? What makes them interested in supporting initiatives that can move museums into new directions? The 2013 TrendsWatch report from American Alliance of Museums looked at the "Changing Shape of Giving."[13] In this report, Merritt of the Center for the Future of Museums highlights the stability of giving (hovering at 2 percent of the GDP even with the swelling number of museums in the U.S.).[14] Optimistic about the stability of giving, Merritt acknowledges the concentration of wealth among Baby Boomers and the need to focus museum attention on this cohort. She also points to the presence of mega donors—certainly a cultivated donor that every museum might love to have in the donor circle. Also looming is the rise of the living mega donor—an individual who acquires a fortune early on and thereby endows early on.

David Callahan examined this changing model of big philanthropy recently.[15] Though these billionaires are not endowing every museum, Callahan identifies a takeaway for us: everything is speeding up: "how fast great wealth is made [and] how fast the bulk of it gets deployed for social purpose." But, if we look at the new models of fundraising, we see that they, too, employ a "fast" mentality. Gone are the days of the year-long build-up to a major stewardship and membership and fundraising event. Those events still happen; but, with greater frequency we see new models of fundraising that exist on the micro and macro levels: microphilanthropy and microgiving are countered by the gift of the crowd (crowdfunding). Is the wisdom of, and funding by, the crowd a wise maneuver? What advantages does it—or other models—have over traditional methods? As we will see in this volume, preparation is key to successful crowdfunding. The lead time and attention is slightly modified (for instance, scripting, dissemination, and engagement with social media across many platforms are critical—perhaps even more so than in a traditional campaign). An additional critical component of the crowdfunded campaign is the need for an authentic connection to one's mission. Because donors may not get to "know" you in real life, crowdfunding campaigns must communicate the message of your organization and this event clearly, effectively, and succinctly!

Statistics show that online giving has grown 13–14 percent year-over-year from 2012 to 2013.[16] Nonetheless, online giving accounted for only 6.4 percent of all charitable giving in 2013. How can museums continue this growth? How can a museum bring "the ask" to places where it isn't already? Tips from funders include suggestions to run campaigns around organizational milestones; to test major campaigns early in the giving year, rather than the end; to implement a monthly giving program; and to mail materials during "slow mail" times. Suggestions were given for online fundraising best practices that can provide insight for all museums. While these seem commonplace, they bear repeating: to embed the donation process inside of your website and ensure that it is device compatible; and, second, to feature a "donate" button on every page of your website. Two less ordinary include a purpose for the "thank you" landing page. Many such click-through pages lack interesting content and rely upon text. By strategically pairing a call to action or a motivation that fits with your mission and vision, you can motivate your donors even further. For instance, if one of your initiatives is to support inclusivity, your thank you can include more ways to become involved in such endeavors local, regionally, or nationally. A second suggestion is to enable tribute gifts or honor donations to celebrate a milestone of another. Such motivation enhances the trust of your donor, and their recipient, have in you by connecting the organization to both individuals.[17] Beyond these best practices, case studies in this volume attest to experiences and successes of authors working with food and drink, public art, and program support. As several authors in this volume attest, bursts of activity, long slumps, and a second wind characterize the ebb-and-flow of the crowdfunded campaign. Yet, an upside is the broadened exposure to your campaign and, even, your museum.

Even with success in fundraising, museums face challenges as they adapt to, and likewise influence, a new and still shifting cultural landscape of the twenty-first century. Just as there is no single approach to fundraising, there is no single pattern for a strategic plan or vision statement. Each much be authentic to an institution and support its collections. For museums come in all shapes, sizes, and types. They teach, inspire, collect, preserve, interpret. They function as community centers and forums for the present, as much as the past and the future. From architecture, archaeology, and art museums to open-air, pop-up, and science museums; from botanic gardens to zoological parks—one size can't fit all.

Moreover, museums exist in a complex and fluid environment that positions them amidst cultural organizations yet also endows them with the responsibility to care for their collections—whether an historic site, a botanic garden, an aquarium, an art museum, a children's museum, a hands-on museum and science center, an art museum, or any variety of nested institutions and organizations (such as archaeology and excavation sites; a resource library in support of a museum and scholarship at large; or a site for public art that serves as a leading public amenity in the nation's largest metropolitan area). How can museum professionals leverage this variety and sustain success?

Fundraising and strategic initiatives are about leadership at all levels—from the museum or site director to the middle-management staff who lead teams of two ore more in the work of museums. Here is where self-awareness, authenticity, courage, and vision are requisite.[18] An example of such courage may be found in the American Alliance of Museums Center for the Future of Museums Extreme Exhibit Makeover held in the spring 2014 at a small museum in Maryland with 3FTE and an operating budget of $385,000. Director Allison Weiss of Sandy Spring Museum, explains, "Our exhibits hadn't changed in fifteen years, and with estimates at $300 a square foot for design and fabrication, building new exhibits was out of the question." [19] Weiss and the institution she directs were able to be brave and nimble. They could experiment and have the trust to give your museum over to two teams of strangers. This is exactly the type of risk a small museum is nimble enough to undertake this kind of activity. For instance, creating a portable exhibit, in the absence of a brick-and-mortar museum, the Museum of Food and Drink under the direction of Peter J. Kim, devised a plan to take a cereal-puffing museum on tour—and to demo it! MOFAD, as you will read in this volume, was brave and nimble (as nimble as can be expected while lugging a 3,200-pound machine around).

Actions such as these require agility on a personal and institutional level. Looking at the needs of our collections, our institution, and our audiences, we have to ask questions at every turn in order to remain relevant, vibrant, and sustainable. Questions include asking how to: program for busy (even if, over-programmed) audiences; differentiate our onsite from online experiences as well as the experiences that we offer in contrast to those that other museums and other options in the marketplace offer; use our resources while making the case for financial support from donors we know (direct, face-to-face, and repeat appeals) and those we do not (and may never) know (such as the ubiquitous crowdfunder). Activities, action, and implementation must be balanced by thinking, planning, and evaluation. Consistent, authentic dialogue among and between colleagues in one's institution as much as peers within one's own city (as Amy Gilman, James G. Leventhal, and Irina Zeylikovich demonstrate in this volume) can strengthen one's own sense of institutional identity. Conversation is key.

Gail Anderson in *Reinventing the Museum: The Evolving Conversation on the Paradigm Shift* (2012) remarks that "reinventing the museum is not just adding a program, reinstalling a gallery, or increasing financial reserves—it is a systemic shift in attitude, purpose, alignment, and execution."[20] It's worth noting that the notion of the "reinvented museum" is not new; Anderson's ideas are informed by earlier iterations of this comparative analysis that she developed and modified in 1998 and 2004.[21] Along with the development of the framework as well as the terms and categories of the characteristics of the reinvented museum, the semantics changed, and I would argue, improved, as well, by moving from a table to a "tool."[22] The notion of a tool indicates measurement and an application to a standard. In thinking about how we think about fundraising and strategic planning, we do measure against a standard. Perhaps the next version of the table will be an digital tool entirely—such as an app that is performance driven, offering some positive re-enforcement (perhaps equally as exciting as reaching a new playable level on the match-three portable device game Candy Crush!) or, even, a "score" for your institution's success at achieving the status of a reinvented museum.

Whatever its form, Anderson's tool deserves considerable examination and, even, discussion; therefore, permit me to bring together some of the content in order to extend her analysis and, thus, introduce the framework for the case studies presented in *Fundraising and Strategic Planning*. According to Anderson, the traditional museum's institutional values offer the voice of authority, conceptualize the institution as the information provider, and project an atmosphere—if not an environment—that is reserved; whereas, the reinvented museum invites multiple viewpoints, serves as a knowledge facilitator, and is compassionate. In terms of governance, Anderson points to the mission as document versus the mission as driver for action; the museum as exclusive or inclusive; the museum as possessing assumed value versus earned value. In terms of management strategy, the traditional museum has a hierarchical structure, unilateral decision-making, compartmentalized goals, and a static role while the reinvented museum is a learning organization that values collective decision-making with holistic, shared goals and strategic positioning. Finally, in terms of communication, the traditional museum is keeper of knowledge versus a platform for the exchange of knowledge; the traditional museum *presents* versus the reinvented museum that *facilitates*; and so on.

The notion of a reinvented museum, then, is really a discussion about how museums of all types and sizes can bear witness to a continued, healthy evolution toward greater transparency and openness in terms of institutional values, governance, management strategies, and communication ideology. As the case studies in *Fundraising and Strategic Planning: Innovative Approaches for Museums* attest, reinventing on a granular level as well as holistic endeavor opens up the space for dialogue among and between staff, audiences, and partner organizations and enables the museum to forge innovative approaches for all.

NOTES

1. Robinson Meyer, "The Museum of the Future is Here," *The Atlantic* January 20, 2015, http://www.theatlantic.com/technology/archive/2015/01/how-to-

build-the-museum-of-the-future/384646/. One of the key developments made possible here is the fusion of an item to a stable home for it on the Internet. The API (application programming interface) associates every item in the collection with a stable URL that permanently anchors it in the collections. The digital and the actual have become linked through the API. Moreover, the API connects the Cooper Hewitt's interface with those of other sites. So, as visitors to Cooper Hewitt's site use the permanent URL, the museum's API will search Flickr, Instagram, and other sites for this link and link back to that site. Thus, the overall presence of Cooper Hewitt grows by harvesting and replicating stable URLs.

2. Cooper Hewitt Labs is the online presence of a group of staff from the Digital & Emerging Media department at Smithsonian's Cooper Hewitt, Smithsonian Design Museum in New York City. Their online archive dates to December 2011, thereby allowing readers the ability to track their initiatives. See "Cooper Hewitt Labs," http://labs.cooperhewitt.org/2011/12/. Working with designer Local Projects, Cooper Hewitt Labs sought answers to questions regarding the visitor experience and how the backend and frontend can serve to answer those questions.

3. Shelley Bernstein, "Visitor Powered Technology to Create a Responsive Museum," *BKM Tech*, September 9, 2014, http://www.brooklynmuseum.org/community/blogosphere/2014/09/09/responsive_museum/.

4. Shelley Bernstein, "Visitor Powered Technology to Create a Responsive Museum," *BKM Tech*, September 9, 2014, http://www.brooklynmuseum.org/community/blogosphere/2014/09/09/responsive_museum/.

5. Bloomberg Philanthropies, "Bloomberg Philanthropies Expands and Rebrands Global Engagement Program," September 9, 2014, http://www.bloomberg.org/press/releases/bloomberg-philanthropies-expands-rebrands-global-engagement-program/.

6. In 2014, $17 million of funding was provided to six institutions through Bloomberg Connects, which provides funding for cultural institutions to enhance visitor experiences through technology. See Bloomberg Philanthropies, "Museums and More Go Digital with Support from Bloomberg Connects" September 9, 2014, http://www.bloomberg.org/blog/museums-go-digital-support-bloomberg-connects/.

7. Jennifer Maloney, "Bloomberg Philanthropies Gives Museums $17 million Push Toward Digital," *The Wall Street Journal* September 8, 2014, http://www.wsj.com/articles/bloomberg-philanthropies-gives-museums-17-million-push-toward-digital-1410226243.

8. For instance, technology and digital initiatives require financial support (as does everything) while informing strategic planning which, in turn, may aim to enhance engagement, access, collections care, and stewardship, among other areas of concentration and action. (Every title of the books in this series is included in the previous sentence.)

9. Cleveland Museum of Art, "Collaborators," http://www.clevelandart.org/gallery-one/collaborators. The statement continues, "The development process was guided by CMA's chief curator and deputy director, Griff Mann-an atypical and noteworthy approach among museums in the design of interactive technology spaces. Museum educators were instrumental in curating the space and its related experiences, and IMTS staff worked closely with internal and external partners on both concept and interactive design. This collaborative organizational structure is groundbreaking, not just within the museum community, but within user-interface

design in general. It elevated each department's contribution, resulting in an un-paralleled interactive experience, with technology and software that has never been used before in any venue, content interpreted in fun and approachable ways, and unprecedented design of an interactive gallery space that integrates technology into an art gallery setting." The site also recognizes their partnership with Local Projects who, under the direction of Jake Barton, designed all of the media and collaborated with the CMA team on concept design development.

10. Mark Stryker, "DIA Supporters Elated by Bankruptcy Decision," *Detroit Free Press*, November 8, 2014, http://www.freep.com/story/entertainment/arts/2014/11/07/dia-elated-bankruptcy-approval/18657133/.

11. Indianapolis Museum of Art, ARTx Fit: Action in Art, http://www.ima museum.org/class/art-x-fit-action-art.

12. National Museum of African American History and Culture, Press Re-lease, July 30, 2014, http://nmaahc.si.edu/content/pdf/Newsroom/NMAAHC_Altria_donation_07302014.pdf. The press release notes that the "museum is scheduled to open in 2016 at a cost of more than $500 mill ion, which covers de-sign, construction and installation of exhibitions. Half the cost is being covered by Congress, the rest by the private sector through a campaign that has raised more than $170 million."

13. See Elizabeth Merritt for the Center for the Future of Museums of the American Alliance of Museums, "TrendsWarch2013: Back to the Future." http://www.aam-us.org/docs/center-for-the-future-of-museums/trendswatch2013.pdf?sfvrsn=4. American Alliance of Museums' Center for the Future of Muse-ums produces groundbreaking work, particularly in the form of the *TrendsWatch* publications that examine trends, connect these to the museum sector, and offer suggestions as to how museums can embrace and, even, adapt these trends.

14. Merritt, 8.

15. David Callahan, "The New WhatsApp Billionaires and the Rise of the Liv-ing Mega Donor," *Inside Philanthropy*, February 24, 2014 http://www.insidephilan thropy.com/home/2014/2/22/the-new-whatsapp-billionaires-and-the-rise-of-the-living-meg.html. The title of Callahan's article takes its cues from WhatsApp, the cross-platform messaging app. The purchase of WhatsApp by Facebook may push the valuation of Facebook to over $100 per share. See Scott Tzu, "WhatsApp Could Push Facebook Over $100," *Seeking Alpha*, January 9, 2015, http://seek ingalpha.com/article/2810015-whatsapp-could-push-facebook-over-100.

16. The 2013 online giving growth was 13.5 percent by Blackbaud Index of Online Giving versus 14 percent from the Network for Good's Online Giving Index. For the report, see "Charitable Giving Report: How NonProfits Per-formed in 2013," Blackbaud. https://www.blackbaud.com/nonprofit-resources/charitablegiving-infographic#.VL7fM0iuJgs and "The Network for Good Digi-tal Giving Index (2013)," Network for Good. http://www1.networkforgood.org/digitalgivingindex. See also The State of Online Giving," June 23, 2013, http://philanthropy.com/article/The-State-of-Online-Giving/139909/#/time. For the summary of tips, see Nonprofit Tech for Good, "10 Online Fundraising Best Practices for Nonprofits," August 24, 2014, http://www.nptechforgood.com/2014/08/24/10-online-fundraising-best-practices-for-nonprofits/.

17. See Nonprofit Tech for Good, "10 Online Fundraising Best Practices for Nonprofits," August 24, 2014, http://www.nptechforgood.com/2014/08/24/10-online-fundraising-best-practices-for-nonprofits/.

18. See Anne W. Ackerson and Joan H. Baldwin, *Leadership Matters*, American Association for State and Local History Series (Lanham, MD: Rowman & Littlefield, 2013). Ackerson and Baldwin note that museum leaders bring many skills to their work and contend that good leadership is personal. Presidents, directors, department heads, and board trustees need to invest in one another, to demonstrate good leadership, and to bear witness to the benefits of mentoring across all levels.

19. Elizabeth Merritt. "Extreme Exhibit Makeover: History Museum Meets Reality TV," *Center for the Future of Museums*, April 1, 2014. Guest post written by Allison Weiss. http://futureofmuseums.blogspot.com/2014/04/extreme-exhibit-makeover-history-museum.html. See https://extremeexhibitmakeover.wordpress.com/ for the blog of the event and the museum's website here: http://www.sandyspringmuseum.org/.

20. Gail Anderson, "Introduction: A Framework," in *Reinventing the Museum: The Evolving Conversation on the Paradigm Shift* (Lanham, MD: AltaMira Press, 2012), 2. The table appears on pages 3 and 4. Anderson explains that "tradition" is not intended to be pejorative but is meant to "illustrate one viewpoint around the museum as institution and concept."

21. See Gail Anderson, *Museum Mission Statements: Building a Distinct Identity* (Washington, D.C.: American Association of Museums Technical Information Service, 1998) and Gail Anderson, *Reinventing the Museum: Historical and Contemporary Perspectives on the Paradigm Shift* (Lanham, MD: AltaMira, 2004). Although fully scrutinizing each iteration of the table (now called a "tool") is beyond the scope of this introduction, mention should be paid to two specific ideas. First is the notion of what the list of terms is and how the list is intended to function. The terms went from being a laundry-list to a "tool"—that is, a device used to carry out a function, in this case the function of the reinvented museum. Though the earlier list of terms was categorized, the positioning of one's own institution seemed more like placement than measurement to a standard. Second, the subtitles of each of these titles give evidence of the shift from traditional to reinvented museum. For instance, "building a distinct identity" demonstrates the way in which a mission statement can inform an institution rather than lead it inquiry, investigation, and work. The 2004 (first edition) of *Reinventing* addresses the role of the historical and the contemporary as ends of a spectrum. The most recent title introduces fluidity and dialogue—aspects of the very social, participatory, and engaged practice of the reinvented museum itself.

22. In the 2012 edition Anderson offers a "Reinventing the Museum Tool" that pairs lists of terms that categorize the traditional museum and the reinvented one.

ONE

BOOM! Crowdfunding the First Exhibit of the Museum of Food and Drink

Peter J. Kim, Museum of Food and Drink

In May 2013, the Museum of Food and Drink (MOFAD) was little more than an idea. We were a small team with a bold vision: we wanted to create a first-of-its-kind museum that explores the culture, history, science, production, and commerce of food and drink—with exhibits you can eat. MOFAD would be a global center for education that inspires people to have a deeper respect for food and make more confident, thoughtful choices.

PLANNING

My team had spent the previous year doing strategic planning and concept development for the museum, and we knew it was time for action. We had acquired the perfect object for our first exhibit: a magnificent, fully functional 3,200-pound machine called the puffing gun. Patented in 1939, this machine had been used by the breakfast cereal industry to heat up ingredients under intense pressure until—*boom!*—they exploded out of the gun's chamber and transformed into crisp, airy puffed cereal.

We knew the puffing gun would be an excellent preview of the future museum's dynamic approach: we would be able to make cereal before visitors' eyes while exploring important themes like breakfast cereal's role in American culture; its surprising history as a religious diet food; the science of pressure, moisture, and puffing; the advent and spread of industrialized food production; and cereal's commercial shift toward sweetened products marketed with sensational colors, jingles, and mascots.

Since we did not have a brick-and-mortar space, we devised a plan to turn the puffing gun into a mobile exhibit called *BOOM! The Puffing Gun*

Figure 1.1. Puffed rice streaks at the camera as the Museum of Food and Drink (MO-FAD) test fires a 1930s-era cereal puffing gun in Brooklyn, New York. MOFAD used Kickstarter, a crowdfunding platform, to raise funding to turn this puffing gun into the traveling exhibit *BOOM! The Puffing Gun and the Rise of Cereal.*

and the Rise of Cereal. We would mount it on a trailer, fabricate transportable exhibit labels, and do live demonstrations of the puffing gun at street fairs and festivals around New York City.

The problem was funding. The estimated cost for exhibit design and fabrication was $80,000. We also needed money for the costs of operating the exhibit. However, as a new and unproven organization, our options were slim. We did not have a developed donor network; we were unwilling to risk compromising our curatorial independence by seek funding from breakfast cereal companies; and it was too late to apply for grants. On top of that, we also wanted to debut the exhibit before the end of the summer. What to do?

Crowdfunding seemed like a good fit. As a budding museum that sought to engage the public in new, exciting ways, we thought it was fitting to fund our first major initiative in an open, collaborative way. We also knew that a successful crowdfunding campaign could generate media attention and build a community of engaged supporters around the project—something we very much needed. Crowdfunding was also consonant with larger trends in individual giving, which showed online donations growing more quickly than overall charitable giving,[1] as well as the millennial generation's preference for social forms of giving that establish a direct link between gifts and concrete outcomes.[2]

We took the plunge. Using an online platform called Kickstarter, we made a video that described our plan and appealed to the public to contribute. And contribute they did. We raised over $106,503 in three hectic weeks from 830 donors around the world, most of whom we did not know at all. The campaign led to coverage in dozens of media outlets, including *The New Yorker, The Wall Street Journal,* Bloomberg TV, and Fast Company. Thousands of people came to see *BOOM!* debut at the New York City Summer Streets festival on August 17, 2013.

This was a bold first step for a nascent organization, and an example of the immense potential of crowdfunding as a fundraising tool for museums. But it was not easy. Our success was the result of careful preparation, around-the-clock promotion, and, frankly, a healthy dose of luck.

Project Timeline

May 1–June 28, 2013
Preparation

June 1
Begin outreach

June 29
Campaign launch

June 30
Day 1: $16,299 raised (13% of goal, average of $16,299/day)

July 2
Day 3: $25,303 raised (32% of goal, average of $8,434/day)

July 7
Day 8: $30,207 raised (38% of goal, average of $3,776/day)

July 11
Day 12: $42,611 raised (53% of goal, average of $3,551/day)

July 17
Day 18: $83,957 raised (105% of goal, average of $4,664/day)

July 20
Campaign end: $106,503 raised (133% of goal, average of $5,072/day)

August 17
Debut of *BOOM!* at the New York City Summer Streets festival

IMPLEMENTATION

Several decisions had to be made with regard to designing and implementing *BOOM! The Puffing Gun and the Rise of Cereal*.

Platform Choice

There are hundreds of crowdfunding platforms with widely varying structures, mechanics, and fees. We decided to use Kickstarter for our campaign, largely because we personally knew several people who had successfully used the platform. We also liked Kickstarter's all-or-nothing system: campaigns that failed to reach their targets received no funding at all. This made failure more costly but increased the likelihood of success. In any event, we needed 100 percent funding to do the exhibit at all, so it made sense to condition our funding on whether we reached our goal.

Campaign Goal

The next matter to resolve was our campaign goal. While our ideal outcome was to net $80,000, the very minimum we needed to raise was $50,000, which would allow us to build a scaled-down version of *BOOM!* We took into consideration reward fulfillment costs (estimated at 30 percent of the gross raise), Kickstarter's fees (5 percent), and credit card processing fees (around 2.2 percent), and calculated that we needed to raise $80,000 to be able to take home $50,000.

But was this feasible? We looked at the history of failed projects on Kickstarter and saw that 81 percent of failed projects did not meet 20 percent of their campaign goal.[3] We called this the 20 percent test and reasoned that if we could pass this threshold in the first couple days of the campaign, we would have an excellent chance of succeeding. We multiplied the number of potential early backers by their estimated conversion rate and the average estimated pledge amount and came up with a number that passed the test. That settled it: our *official* campaign goal was $80,000.

Preparation

We began preparing about two months prior to the campaign launch date. In addition to scripting, shooting, and producing our pitch video, as well as drafting the copy of our project page, we knew that pledge level optimization was a critical component of successful crowdfunding. Optimization refers to setting the default giving levels at the right increments and creating an appropriate value proposition to potential donors at each level.

We researched Kickstarter data and comparable projects and came to the following conclusions:

- Most successful campaigns had at least seven pledge levels.[4]
- In terms of quantity, pledges between $11 and $100 were the most active categories on Kickstarter in 2011, accounting for 71.9 percent of all pledges.
- Above $100 and below $11, pledge quantity dropped off significantly; the drop was much more pronounced for pledges greater than $100.
- However, most of the money raised by Kickstarter campaigns came from the middle and high level tiers, with pledges from $51 to $500 generating the most funding.[5]

One important takeaway was that while low-level pledges were not the biggest source of funding, they were not to be neglected. We noted that crowdfunding campaigns were fueled by viral sharing—i.e., supporters sharing the campaign with their own contacts and social networks, drawing more contributions from new supporters who also share the campaign, and so on. As such, it was critical to maximize the sheer quantity of campaign participants by creating attractive lower level pledge levels.

We observed that successful nonprofit crowdfunding projects typically described the advantages of giving in two ways: (1) the donation's impact on the organization's work, e.g., "provide one hour of nutrition education to one student by donating $20," and (2) benefits given back to the donor, e.g., "receive a mug by donating $10." In our case, we found it difficult to segment *BOOM!* development into discrete portions. So we highlighted the more global goal of creating MOFAD's first exhibit. To optimize our individual pledge levels, we needed to offer unique, meaningful donor benefits that proportionately scaled up in value.

As an entry point, donors who gave $10 had their names published on the mofad.org website and also received exclusive updates from us. We intentionally did not offer anything tangible. We knew that pledge quantity typically spiked at levels higher than $10, so it made sense to encourage people to donate a bit more by offering our first physical reward at $30: a beautifully designed t-shirt. We also created a tier at $50, offering a sturdy, recycled tote bag with "food is culture" written in nine different languages.

We paid special attention to the $100 to $500 range. Suspecting that these levels might account for the majority of the money raised by the campaign, we considered them our campaign's "flagship" tiers. Given the relatively large leap from $50 to these levels, we offered one-of-a-kind rewards that tied directly into the puffing gun concept. For $100, donors received puffed snacks fired from the puffing gun. It was also the first level at which donors received both the t-shirt and the tote. At $300 and up, donors were invited to an exhibit preview party featuring star chefs using the puffing gun. This was an opportunity to see the exhibit before anyone else and to mingle with well-known personalities from the culinary world.

We had some doubts about our ability to draw bigger donations but, figuring that it could only be to our benefit, we created tiers all the way up to $10,000 (the maximum allowed on Kickstarter). At these levels, we relaxed our strict cost-benefit analysis and offered rewards that involved special, individualized attention, like private exhibit showings and a custom cereal line.

Outreach

As a relatively unknown organization with only a small network of supporters, we knew that outreach was a top priority. We started about one month in advance of the campaign launch, and focused our energy on three important groups: (1) personal contacts, (2) people with large followings, or "influencers," and (3) media outlets.

Personal Contacts

For these contacts, we took care to encourage personal investment in the project. We did this by sending out regular correspondence, involving contacts in the creative process, soliciting feedback, and inviting them to a campaign launch party. At the campaign launch party, we served a homemade dinner, spoke about our vision for the project, screened our Kickstarter video, officially launched the campaign, and then asked everyone in the room to make a pledge using one of the computers we had set up.

One tool we found quite useful for taking stock of our personal networks was Gmail's automatically generated contact database—it keeps track of people with whom you have had repeated correspondence. We used an online application called Boomerang to pre-write emails and schedule them for delivery, which allowed us to spend evenings writing emails for daytime delivery, freeing up the most important hours of the day.

We created a simple, easily remembered web address, boom.mofad. org, that redirected visitors to our Kickstarter page. This was particularly helpful when orally telling people about the campaign. We also created a press dashboard, launch.mofad.org, that allowed our supporters to easily "like" our press coverage thereby increasing its visibility.

Influencers

Given our mission, we figured that we would be most likely to find influencers in the culinary industry. We managed to get Mario Batali, Cesare Casella, David Chang, Wylie Dufresne, Brooks Headley, and Anita Lo to vouch for us in our pitch video. In so doing, they became engaged in the project and also helped us get the word out to their networks. Having well-known personalities involved in our campaign also proved helpful for our media pitches.

In addition, we used the online tools Klout and followerwonk to analyze our social media followers, enabling us to prioritize the most influential people in our network. We asked our top social media influencers to help us by sharing our campaign.

Media Outlets

We created a prioritized list of media contacts we wanted to pitch, placing equal weight on each outlet's reach and likelihood of covering our campaign. This naturally led us to focus on food and drink blogs. We also looked for people who could make personal introductions. For this, Facebook and LinkedIn were immensely helpful for identifying mutual contacts. For media contacts with whom we did not have a personal connection, we sent personal emails with press releases. One tool that we found highly useful for writing a lot of emails was a "text expander" that allowed us to easily insert chunks of stock language.

The Campaign

Nearly universally, Kickstarter campaigns follow a pattern. They begin with a burst of activity and then slow down into a prolonged slump before reenergizing as the deadline approaches. Our campaign was no exception. Right out of the gate, we raised 32 percent of our goal in the first three days. Despite this promising start, we hit the July 4 holiday and campaign activity stopped nearly altogether. On July 6, we raised only $201, and on July 10, we limped over the 50 percent funding mark. We were not on pace to meet our campaign target.

We redoubled our efforts and did everything we could. We sent thousands of emails, made hundreds of phone calls, pitched media, pitched social media influencers, organized an online question-and-answer session on Twitter, and we asked all of our supporters to reach out to their own personal networks. Through sheer force of will, we built momentum back up. On the morning of July 17, we woke up to see that MOFAD had surpassed the campaign goal. We were on our way to launching our first exhibit.

RESULTS

Our campaign was a success. In addition to raising $106,503 on Kick-starter—which was well beyond our $80,000 target—we raised nearly $30,000 offline from donors who did not want to pay by credit card. The overall raised was over $136,000, or 170 percent of our campaign goal. At the time (July 2013), we were the most highly funded museum project in the history of Kickstarter.

Looking at our campaign results in more detail, we observed that our pledge level strategy worked quite well. As predicted, our lower tiers drew the greatest level of participation while our mid-level tiers raised the most money. To our surprise, we managed to attract a handful of bigger donors—their comparatively larger contributions had a significant effect on the campaign. In other words, we had created value out of all parts of the pledge spectrum.

Our investment in our personal contacts was the single most important aspect of our outreach strategy. Our friends and family were the biggest champions of the project. They acted as force multipliers by making heartfelt, personal appeals to their own networks—the results of which were reflected in our campaign referral statistics. Fully 47 percent of the money raised came via direct traffic, which means the donor entered the campaign page web address directly into the browser or clicked on a link, meaning that these donors were obtained by email and other personal

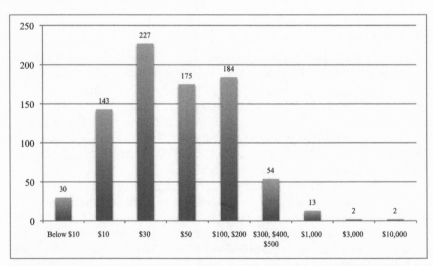

Figure 1.2.   The number of donors at each pledge level at the conclusion of MOFAD's 2013 *BOOM!* Kickstarter campaign. Certain pledge levels are grouped because they offered similar rewards.

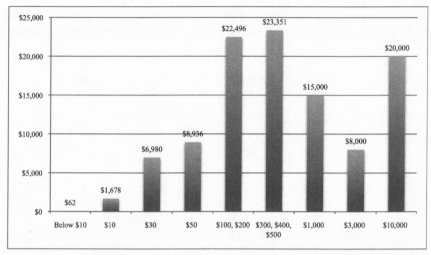

Figure 1.3.   The amount of money raised by each pledge level at the conclusion of MO-FAD's 2013 *BOOM!* Kickstarter campaign. Certain pledge levels are grouped because they offered similar rewards.

communication. On the other hand, only 12 percent of donations resulted from people discovering our campaign through the Kickstarter platform. I obtained similar data from other Kickstarter campaigns and found similar results, though social media referral rates were typically higher than ours.

Perhaps the biggest benefit to MOFAD was increased exposure. We tallied over thirty press hits and had created a broad, engaged audience for the exhibit. Many of these backers visited *BOOM!* as we toured it around New York City. It was immensely satisfying to finally meet our donors face-to-face and show them what we had built with the money they had contributed and raised.

LESSONS LEARNED

MOFAD's campaign may have been successful but it was chaotic, stressful, and exhausting. Moreover, the campaign monopolized the entire team's attention and everything else at MOFAD ground to a halt.

In retrospect, I would have taken at least one more month to prepare. We spent too much time playing catch-up on correspondence during the campaign. I would have had most of our communications prewritten, along with a detailed outreach calendar planned out in advance. With such tasks completed ahead of time, we could have run a much more stress-free, effective crowdfunding campaign while also working on other aspects of MOFAD.

Another weak point of our campaign was the middle "slump" phase, during which our momentum was nearly lost. We should have been prepared for this. We could have, for example, created a short video series to maintain interest during the "slump." Or, we could have orchestrated a coordinated social media campaign during that period. We are lucky to have picked up speed again. Given the opportunity, I would have had several of these "boost" strategies ready to go.

DRILLING DOWN: WHAT'S NEXT?

Taking into account the time spent preparing the campaign, running it, and then fulfilling rewards, crowdfunding may not be the most time-efficient form of fundraising. Moreover, it is not an effective strategy for seeking donations from older donors who are less familiar with social media and online giving.

However, MOFAD will always consider crowdfunding when launching a new program, primarily because a well-executed campaign can create a sense of community and reach new audiences in a way that traditional fundraising cannot do. The flip side of this ability to generate excitement is that it is necessary to space out crowdfunding campaigns. In the future, we will save it for only our most compelling projects.

There is one project in particular that I look forward to crowdfunding one day: the first brick-and-mortar home for the Museum of Food and Drink. It doesn't get much more exciting than that.

NOTES

1. Sharf, Samantha. "Charitable Giving Grew 4.9% In 2013 As Online Donations Picked Up." Forbes. February 5, 2014. Accessed November 14, 2014. http://www.forbes.com/sites/samanthasharf/2014/02/05/charitable-giving-grew-in-2013-as-online-giving-picked-up/.

2. Rowner, Mark. *The Next Generation of American Giving: The Charitable Habits of Generations Y, X, Baby Boomers, and Matures.* Edited by Dennis McCarthy and Michael Johnston. Charleston, South Carolina: Blackbaud, 2013. 25.

3. "Distribution of Unsuccessfully Funded Projects on Crowdfunding Platform Kickstarter as of July 2014, by Share of Funding Reached." Statista. July 1, 2014. Accessed November 14, 2014. http://www.statista.com/statistics/251732/overview-of-unsuccessfully-funded-projects-on-crowdfunding-platform-kickstarter/.

4. Neel, Michael. "Kickstarter Stats You Can Use." ViNull.com. July 25, 2012. Accessed November 14, 2014. http://www.vinull.com/2012/07/25/kickstarter-stats-you-can-use/.

5. Strickler, Yancey, and Fred Benenson. "One Million Backers." Kickstarter Blog. October 11, 2011. Accessed November 14, 2014. https://www.kickstarter.com/blog/one-million-backers.

TWO

Public Art and Public Support

A New Direction at the
Carnegie Center for Art & History

Karen Gillenwater,[1]
Carnegie Center for Art & History

PLANNING

In mid-2008, when I joined the staff of the Carnegie Center for Art & History, the center's director, Sally Newkirk, and I began brainstorming ideas to place public art around our location in downtown New Albany, Indiana. We recognized from the beginning that one of our main hurdles would be finding the resources, in both time and funds, to present such a project. However, because of the Carnegie Center's history of presenting innovative visual art since 1971 and our awareness that public art would help us to engage more of the underserved residents of our city, we felt that it was imperative that we find a way to make this idea a reality. As a small organization with four full-time staff members, we knew that we would need to take a creative approach to many aspects of this project, including fundraising.

Fortunately, we received an unexpected boost in the form of a letter from Michael Ladd, executive director of the New Albany Urban Enterprise Association (UEA), with an invitation to partner with the UEA to place public art in the city. Each organization pledged $25,000 for public art and together we organized the New Albany Public Art Project: Bicentennial Series. Lasting from 2010–2013, this series presented fifteen temporary artworks that included a wide range of artistic approaches and media, while bringing to life aspects of our city's history. This series was conceived with the goals of involving the entire community in celebrating our diverse history and promoting an appreciation of contemporary art, educating the public by highlighting local history and art venues, promoting economic development in downtown New Albany and enticing individuals who are interested in history to experience contemporary art and vice versa.

Tasklist

• Established a relationship and common goals with our partner organization, the New Albany Urban Enterprise Association (UEA).
• The board of directors for each partner organization committed $25,000 in
start up funds toward the project.
• Applied for and secured a grant from a local foundation to fund the first
year of the project.
• Initiated the project by inviting organizations and individuals with which
we had a positive relationship to host artworks on their properties.
• Planned personal interactions with the artists for stakeholders and the public to generate engagement and support.
• Acted on the opportunity to raise funds through unique experiences and
public events.
• Maintained awareness of new methods of fundraising and adopted them
when it was appropriate for our project.
• Sought methods to increase community engagement and public involvement in the project.
• Developed innovative ways for the public to learn about the artworks and
interact with the project during events and programs.
• Completed regular evaluations of the project to measure success and make
adjustments to the project.

IMPLEMENTATION

With start-up funds in place, we strategized ways to raise the additional
funds from external sources. We first secured a grant from a local foundation to reach the income requirement for the first project year. In the end,
$64,500 of the total four-year project budget of $136,000 would be raised
through grant funds. We began the project by building on the relationships that the Carnegie Center had developed by inviting organizations,
business owners, and individuals with whom we had positive relationships to host artworks on their properties. This enabled us to work with
entities that were open to new ideas and that trusted our organizational
capacity, which ensured that we could present innovative artworks. The
in-kind support of these property owners should not be undervalued, as
it was pivotal to our ability to build enthusiasm and financial support for
the project within the community.

Because this project was the first of its kind in our city, we were mindful of providing opportunities for the public to learn about the artworks.
Personal interactions with the artists proved to be a valuable tool for generating in-kind and financial sponsorships for the project as well as public

engagement. The selection process in the first year yielded three works with traditional materials of metal, concrete, and glass as well as a video projection by Valerie Sullivan Fuchs and a sculpture made out of recycled materials by Leticia Bajuyo. Since the owners of the sites for artwork were providing essential in-kind support for the project, we informed them first about the selections. There were some surprised responses, particularly to the video projection because of its lack of physical form. Fortunately, our timing was perfect, as both Valerie Sullivan Fuchs and Leticia Bajuyo had solo exhibitions of their work on view in nearby Louisville, Kentucky. They gave tours of their exhibitions to the site owners and members of the staff and boards of directors of the partner organizations. Those who attended were inspired by their experience interacting with these artists and became fervent supporters of the project. This led us to plan an invitation-only breakfast with key personnel including project artists, staff, board members, site owners as well as elected officials, potential sponsors, colleagues from the art community and the media. After this event, we not only had several new pledges of financial and in-kind support, but we also had developed a group of community members who became advocates for the project and helped to build interest in the artworks.

The second year of our project witnessed the selection of an audio installation by local artist Scott Scarboro. After experiencing the video projection as public art the year before, our community greeted the announcement of the audio installation with enthusiasm. This particular piece also resulted in a unique fundraising opportunity. The installation was created to interpret the historic theme of newspapers and broadcasting. Bob Edwards, former host of National Public Radio's *All Things Considered* and *Morning Edition* got his start in radio in 1968 at the local radio station WHEL. Scott Scarboro contacted Mr. Edwards and convinced him not only to record audio segments to be incorporated into the art installation, but to also visit the Carnegie Center during his upcoming book tour.[2] Edwards was generous with his time, enabling us to raise funds for the Public Art Project during an interview attended by over one hundred people. In addition, we auctioned a private dinner for twelve with Edwards. Indeed, such unique experiences and brushes with celebrity can be powerful fundraisers.

New fundraising ideas can come from outside sources as well. In 2010, Randy Smith and Ann Baumgartle, owners of a local bookstore, presented us with the idea of hosting a reading marathon and fundraiser for the project during a Thanksgiving weekend event. They asked members of the community to sign up for thirty-minute time slots to read aloud in their store. The volunteers in turn gathered pledges of $1.00 per minute for the time that they read with all proceeds going to the project. Thanks to the efforts of the storeowners and the volunteers and the enthusiasm of the community, $1,100 was raised. In advance of the reading relay, Amy Gesenhues, columnist for the local *News and Tribune* wrote an article that emphatically expressed the value of public art and generated interest in the fundraiser:

> Often times, art and business are put into separate categories; as if they are two distinctly different areas of our culture; as if art's only job in relation to business is to adorn the walls of corporate buildings. We fail to recognize that art does more than inspire more art. Art can inspire the creative urge that results in new business ideas in the same way as it inspires new pieces of art. The spark that ignites the next great commerce idea is the same as the spark that delivers the next great American novel. In times like these, when innovation is so crucial to our economic survival, public art is needed more than ever.[3]

As our project evolved so did fundraising methods and we particularly saw the rise of crowdfunding. We felt this could be an appropriate method to raise funds for public art from the community. Our goal was to raise the amount of the artist's honorarium for one of the artworks to be installed in the spring of 2011. We chose to give each donor of $1.00 or more the opportunity to vote on which of that year's artworks would be designated as funded by the community thus affirming that community input and dialogue were as important as the funds we would raise. We selected to launch a campaign through Indiegogo because we would receive the funds that were pledged regardless of whether we met our fundraising goal.[4] This turned out to be very valuable since we did not meet our goal. However, the funds that we did raise helped us to reach our overall goal and the campaign introduced the project to new donors. This was also a valuable experience for our staff as it led us to increase our social media presence and our use of video, both of which have helped us to reach new audiences and develop new ways for our audiences to engage with art. We did not give up on crowdfunding; however, and launched a Power2Give.org campaign to help fund the 2012 art installations.[5] Fortunately, through expanded social media efforts and increased involvement of our board of directors, we reached our fundraising goal for this campaign. Members of our board of directors made significant personal donations to the crowdfunding campaigns and also assisted with fundraising by introducing us to local business representatives and individuals who became financial supporters of the project.

Successful organizations often demonstrate an ability to adapt the techniques of others to reach their goals. When I attended the 2011 National Folk Festival in Nashville, Tennessee, I was impressed by the way that they collected donations from attendees in a way that improved upon the experience. This free event, organized by the National Council for the

Traditional Arts, celebrates the wide range of traditional arts that are part of American culture. Between the stages, workshop tents and exhibits roamed a corps of friendly volunteers wearing bright red cowboy hats and holding orange buckets. These members of the "Bucket Brigade" were collecting donations. Rather than instilling a plea from the brigade and guilt or avoidance from attendees, the "ask" took the form of an onstage host reminding the crowd to support the free event by "making a drop in the bucket." An additional stroke of brilliance was the distribution of a sticker given to donors as a means of acknowledging their gift. The volunteers had the happy job of thanking each person who passed wearing a sticker and, as an attendee, one felt even more a part of the event.

We adopted this concept for our New Albany Public Art Walk in 2012. During this free event, attendees roam downtown, visiting the public art sites to see the art and talk with the artists. Throughout the Public Art Walk route visitors participate in various activities, including screen-printing a poster inspired by the artworks, learning about the annual themes and watching dramatic performances by high-school theater students. We interspersed our own "Bucket Brigade" volunteers between the activities and asked them to make visitors feel welcome, hand out maps and, of course, give stickers to and thank those who gave donations in their buckets. Because our event is located in the shopping and restaurant district and one of our goals was to encourage attendees to patronize local businesses, the stickers had an added benefit in that they provided a visual indicator to the business owners of the many customers that the event brought to them—as did the t-shirts and reusable bags that visitors could purchase to show their support for public art at other times. The only complaint we received was from volunteers who said their buckets were too light because visitors they encountered often had stickers. Thus, our volunteers spent the evening thanking people for already giving—a point that we saw, of course, as a measure of success!

RESULTS

Developed under a partnership between the Carnegie Center and the UEA, the New Albany Public Art Project has resulted in fifteen diverse public art installations that have encouraged dialogue about contemporary art and given residents and civic leaders an expanded concept of what art can be and its importance in a community. We measure the success of the project through surveys and feedback gathered from the public and other stakeholders. These evaluations have demonstrated that we are meeting the project goals and have also aided us in improving the project. We have seen an increase in our community's engagement with art. One visitor wrote in her survey response: "You have inspired my interest in the arts! Future tense!" It was gratifying for us to see our community's concept of public art expand over the years of the project from one focused on figurative, monumental sculpture to one that includes ephemeral artworks and new media installations. The artworks and the opportunities visitors had to interact with the artists resonated deeply with members of our community, as evidenced in the following visitor comment: "These artworks add to the beauty and sense of New Albany being a with-it community. Many of the pieces provoke discussion and contemplation and that is what art is supposed to do." We could not have provided these positive experiences to our community without the generous sponsors who supported this project both financially and with in-kind donations.

LESSONS LEARNED

What began as a goal among the staff at the Carnegie Center to bring art to more members of our community, has grown through collaboration and support from many individuals into a project that has been recognized as an innovative approach to the presentation of both art and history. Though we are proud of the recognition that this project has received from others, we are even more proud that it has remained relevant to the residents of New Albany. Maintaining a focus on our community and the goals of the project has enabled us to continue to present this program and to have a positive impact on the individuals who experience the artworks. These personal connections have also been a significant factor in our success in raising the funds necessary to continue to present innovative public art in New Albany.

DRILLING DOWN: WHAT'S NEXT?

Because of the importance of this project, we published a catalogue of the Bicentennial Series artworks and historic themes. To continue to make these accessible to all of our community, the printed catalogue is available for a suggested donation and a digital version is available online as a free download.[6] All catalogue donations will support a second public art series, to be presented by the Carnegie Center for Art & History. In this way, the catalogue not only documents the success of the first series and recognizes the significant contributions of the project supporters, but it also sets the foundation for future innovations. The New Albany

Public Art Project: Today & Tomorrow Series will bring new artworks to New Albany interpreting themes that impact the city today—sustainability, education and literacy, the arts and design, diversity and human rights, and social change. In the spirit of collaboration with which the public art project began, we involved the community in the selection of these themes and we are collaborating with organizational colleagues to provide educational opportunities and to create community conversations about how we can respond to these ideas to make our city a better place in the future. We strive to share our resources and expertise with colleagues both near and far to encourage others to build upon what we have accomplished.

RESOURCES

Americans for the Arts Public Art Network. http://www.americansforthearts
.org/by-program/networks-and-councils/public-art-network.
Goldstein, Barbara, ed., *Public Art by the Book*. Washington: University of Wash- ·
ington Press, 2005.
Public Art Dialogue. Semiannual. Abingdon, UK: Taylor & Francis.
Public Art Review. Semiannual. St. Paul, MN: FORECAST Public Art.

NOTES

1. Karen Gillenwater served as curator at the Carnegie Center for Art & History before taking up the position of museum manager at 21c Museum Hotel in Louisville, Kentucky.

2. Selections from Scott Scarboro's *Time Ghost tower-casts #1 and #2* and video of an interview with Bob Edwards can be accessed at: https://www.youtube.com/user/TheCarnegieCenter.

3. Amy Gesenhues, "Please, please, please give to the public arts program (please)," *News and Tribune*, November 24, 2010.

4. Carnegie Center for Art & History, "New Albany Public Art Project: Bicentennial Series," https://www.indiegogo.com/projects/new-albany-public-art-project-bicentennial-series.

5. Carnegie Center for Art & History, "New Albany Public Art Project: Bicentennial Series," http://www.power2give.org/kentucky/Project/Detail?projectId=744.

6. Download the New Albany Public Art Project: Bicentennial Series catalogue at: http://www.carnegiecenter.org.

THREE

Crowdfunding the Museum

*Engaging Program Constituents in
Resource Development*

Melissa A. Russo,
Chabot Space & Science Center

Chabot Space & Science Center, founded in 1883, is a nonprofit interactive science center with a mission to inspire and educate students of all ages about planet Earth and the universe. Nestled in thirteen acres of East Bay Regional Park land in the hills of Oakland, California, the current facility opened in 2000 and features 85,000 square feet of interactive astronomy, space travel and climate science exhibits, a full dome planetarium, and massive telescopes open to the public. Welcoming over 170,000 visitors a year, the center's activities include public programs and exhibits, school field trips, science camps, teacher training, after school teen programs and community outreach.

Like all museums, the center struggles with maintaining and growing a robust stream of contributed revenue. Built largely with federal earmarks and other government funds (which were relatively plentiful in the late 1990s), the center fell victim to a board and staff that over-relied on this single source to build and maintain programs and operations. As government funding took a severe downturn in the recession, the center activated strategies to build capacity in other areas of fundraising.

PLANNING

With a strategic goal of broadening the center's core donor base, the development team looked to new technologies in 2011–2012. Crowdfunding, a new social networking and fundraising phenomenon, was one of the most promising tools the team wanted to research and implement. Crowdfunding takes advantage of online crowd-based decision-making and, through any one of a number of dedicated websites, taps into the social networks of individuals to bring in donations. To varying degrees, crowdfunding platforms bring their own followers to the effort, but fundamentally, successful campaigns rely on the organization's ability to leverage concentric circles of social networks that are comfortable with transactions online.

The annual unrestricted contributed revenues of the center are about $2.5 million, nearly half of the overall budget of the organization. The majority of gifts from individuals are realized as unrestricted gifts from the September fundraising gala and at year end. The demographic of these regular donors[1]—older, retired, and somewhat disconnected from the direct services and programming at the center, which targets younger families—made this group a less than ideal cohort for our foray into social media fundraising. Moreover, our review of the research indicated that individuals aged twenty-four to thirty-five were most likely to back crowdfunding campaigns. This demographic was sorely lacking in our donor profiles. Interestingly, research also indicated that African Americans, Asians, and Latinos were more likely to participate than Caucasians in crowdfunding efforts.[2] Such research was positive for us, since our efforts aimed to diversify and expand our donor network. In addition, like most museums and science centers, Chabot has hundreds of adult and teen volunteers.[3] Because each of them has their own unique networks, these volunteers represent a community which is visibly more diverse in age and ethnicity than our existing donor base. Thus, the prospect of activating existing, but untapped volunteer constituencies was intriguing.

IMPLEMENTATION

All crowdfunding efforts essentially follow the same process:

1. Campaign team has an idea that needs funding.
2. Team picks a crowdfund platform; registers the campaign (requiring a contact person and bank account information where proceeds can be transferred).
3. Rewards and incentives are developed.
4. Team writes a short and appealing description of the project that indicates the organization's need for funds, lists rewards for various levels of giving, and provides the deadline for pledges.[4]
5. Team shares case statement with a circle of supporters who will be the "sharers" of the project. Team allows for feedback or customization from this group as possible.
6. Photos and video(s) are produced to provide compelling visuals for the campaign and to demonstrate results throughout the campaign.
7. Project is submitted/uploaded to the crowdfund website.

8. Project webpage is launched (goes live); team shares with circle of supporters who, in turn, share via emails and social media (Facebook, Twitter, Instagram).

9. Team posts several times weekly to the crowdfund comment feed in order to give updates, encouragement, and thank you to donors. Posts and links are made on social media pages and are shared beyond the crowdfund page.

10. Campaign concludes. Individual donors are publicly thanked on the comment feed. Rewards are distributed and formal donor acknowledgments are sent.

When choosing a platform, it's important to realize that your campaign will be shared not just with and by your circle of supporters but also the host site also brings their followers who are, in turn, potential donors that you may tap.

Some of the crowdfunding platforms that command larger shares of the market are: Kickstarter, GoFundMe, Crowdrise, Razoo, Donors Choose, and Indiegogo. About 71 percent of the current sites are based on the donation/philanthropy/sponsorship model[5] and some sites are devoted to lending (microfinancing) rather than donation-based philanthropy.

Two challenges needed to be resolved: the audience for this campaign and the right platform. As mentioned, our existing donor list was not the right demographic for a crowdfund. In addition, staff wanted to avoid "cannibalizing" the current donor list for project funding if that meant that donors might give to this crowdfund *instead* of giving to our annual fund. We wanted to identify an alternative circle of fundraisers and/or donors that our campaign would rely on to build the concentric circles of supporters that we needed for our campaign to be a success.

In terms of the platform, Chabot's staff devoted time to familiarizing themselves with the projects on various sites, making it readily apparent what communities would more likely embrace our nonprofit, science education-based project. Meanwhile, in Chabot's backyard, an online fundraising platform was gaining appeal. Piggybackr is devoted exclusively to raising funds for youth programs and utilizing the volunteer fundraising efforts of the youth themselves. Because the Piggybackr staff knew of our youth programs, Chabot was given the opportunity to launch our crowdfund campaign and participate in the early testing of the site while in beta in 2012 (Piggybackr was co-founded by Andrea Lo and Keenahn Jung). Thus, the circle of supporters—our youth—and the platform—Piggybackr—had been resolved. The next step was to tap into the perfect group of youth to engineer the project and to achieve its success.

Figure 3.1. Piggybackr is a crowdfund website devoted exclusively to raising funds for youth programs and to utilizing the volunteer fundraising efforts of the youth themselves. Over the two campaigns, donors gave 81 gifts in 2013 and 152 gifts in 2014. These donors were nearly all first-time givers.

Chabot's Galaxy Explorers

For the last fifteen years, Chabot has conducted a teen volunteer program called the Galaxy Explorers (GE). A weekly high touch program, GE enrolls 130 active high school students in free-of-charge sessions where they take classes, engage in team activities, projects, and lectures. The teens, in turn, serve as paid intern science explainers performing science demonstrations for the public visitors. Participants in the program gain a life-long connection to science, work experience, and community service/volunteer hours while learning organizational skills. The GE program cultivates continuous enrollment and sustained involvement from the participants. Many GEs were passionate about their experiences and commitment to the program, having started as young as seventh grade in the middle school Champions of Science program and continuing until high school graduation. Yet, they had never organized a fundraiser. As volunteers, they were already engaged in talking about their Chabot experience with family and friends, so the group was the right constituency to help with our crowdfund effort. We decided to launch the fundraiser in February 2013, a lull in the school calendar. The duration of the campaign was five weeks from launch to conclusion—which is swift in comparison to other fundraising campaigns. However, crowdfund campaigns seem to be most successful when they are of short duration.

On the Piggybackr site, registration and set up of the "master page" took about two hours. The page was approved within forty-eight hours. Then we met with our students to orient participants and gauge their knowledge of fundraising and social media marketing. We created a Powerpoint presentation to walk them through creating their own unique custom pages which would, in turn, link to the main page. Students had about ten days to pull together their own pages. Some students used our template language and added a photo of themselves engaged in the program, other students got very creative with their messages and pages. While the overall fundraiser had a goal of $15,000, each student posted an individual goal, averaging about $200. Once the pages were done, each student was asked to send at least twenty emails to a circle of family and friends that would provide a link back to the individual's crowdfund page. In addition, students could share the link on Facebook, Instagram, Twitter, and other social media.

Similar to traditional fundraising campaigns, donors were incentivized with "rewards" at various tiers. We were careful to keep these fun and relatively modest because crowdfund campaigns rely more on donor emotion and feeling of "doing good," rather than what they will get in return for their donation. For instance, at the modest $50 "Asteroid" level, donors were given a big thank you, email updates, and a shout out on Facebook and at the high $1,000 level donors were offered all the above plus a one-year membership to the center.

Successful crowdfund campaigns rely on creating excitement and urgency for the cause. During the course of the campaign, it was important for us to send periodic messages of encouragement to the students, which in turn impacted the success of the message reaching donors. This ripple effect kept energy going throughout the five weeks. Our experience mirrored that in the crowdfund industry: in the week after launch we received about 25 percent of the total donations, presumably from those donors immediately reacting to the message. As team leader on the Piggybackr site for this project, we at Chabot were able to send messages to all donors to instruct them to share the campaign more widely. Most gratifying were the donations from former alums of the GE program who suddenly re-engaged with us. Once they had been reached, and in turn, their social network had been tapped by youth, the GE alums came out of the woodwork and participated in the campaign. This constituency had previously not been successfully reached by Chabot's development team. Donations from the GE alums included statements such as: "The GE program has helped opened my eyes to the world, opens potential career fields, and gives people opportunities to change the world in ways that weren't otherwise possible."

RESULTS

At the conclusion of the 2013 campaign, 71 percent of the $15,000 goal was reached and posted on the campaign page.[6] In 2014, the goal was increased to $20,000 and the students raised 56 percent of that goal. In fact, with triple the number of students participating the second year (85 vs 24), slightly fewer funds were raised ($10,495 in 2013 vs. $10,687 in 2014). Two reasons are proposed for this outcome. The 2013 group of students included two high school seniors whose families donated substantially larger amounts to their fundraiser than the average gifts, positively skewing the results. Also, the largest percentage of 2013 participants were students on the Galaxy Explorers Astronomy Team–students motivated by a Hong Kong Space Museum travel exchange project which, in turn, greatly motivated their fundraising efforts.

Over the two campaigns, donors gave 81 gifts in 2013 (average $132) and 152 gifts in 2014 (average $69). These donors were almost entirely first-time givers. In calculating the response rate of our efforts, we benchmarked against acquisition response rates. Within that context, our 4.6 percent response rate was better than the direct mail industry average response rate that hovers around 1 percent.

Other measurements held equal or more value than the numeric results—namely, the number of people touched by and responding to the message. Over the two campaigns, 109 students sent 5,000 emails to their networks, an average of 45 for each student. In addition, and uncalculated, students used other social media outlets to tell about the campaign.

About 30,000 page views, which included family and friends of the students branching out further to their networks, were logged on the Piggybackr site. The promotional value in this number of introductions was truly priceless, and the contact information collected provided further opportunity for outreach after the campaign was over.

By expanding our donor reach through this crowdfund campaign, Chabot received gifts after the crowdfund concluded, some of which were designated for other purposes. For instance, a GE family sponsored a $10,000 gala table and also gave generously through the auction. By the fall of 2014, these additive contributions added up to nearly $50,000.

LESSONS LEARNED

Utilizing youth volunteers served as an ideal entrée into this fundraising environment. No other constituency could make a case for the program as effectively or advocate so authentically as the students who were the direct benefactors, and the students felt a great sense of accomplishment in participating in a philanthropic team project.

One of the revelations of the process was how effective it could be to cultivate communities not traditionally prospected. The potential for going beyond the board of director's network and tapping into the networks of all of our stakeholders is really the most compelling result of our experience. Student program participants, docent volunteers, museum members, and museum neighbors are not traditionally stakeholders utilized on a broad scale in fundraising; but, undoubtedly, they all have an interest in seeing the museum succeed.

In providing our students the framework and tools to share their passion, we learned that specificity and transparency about the project or program was key. Description, process, challenges, and results were important elements to include in the messaging and updates. In our preparation, we made sure to allow for collateral like photos and imagery—all of which could be produced by the staff or students. Data is good to share, but images are of immense importance, especially short clip videos (under one minute) featuring the students.

DRILLING DOWN: WHAT'S NEXT?

The crowdfund model will not replace traditional fundraising practices of face-to-face cultivation and stewardship in soliciting major gifts from high net worth individuals. Yet, one of the great promises of crowdfunding is that it promotes philanthropy beyond the traditional wealthy donor, allowing for broader public awareness and inclusion in giving. Studies indicate that crowdfunding practices will expand as tech-saavy millennials age into our primary donor base. A recent report claims that in 2013 millennials represented about 11 percent of total giving, and a high percentage, "62 percent of millennials gave through mobile platforms—and tended to learn about charities via their peers."[7]

With minimal barriers to entry, and potential for introducing organizations to new funders and friends, crowdfunding promises to be an increasingly valuable tool for the museum and science center fundraising community. At Chabot Space & Science Center, we have institutionalized our Galaxy Explorer crowdfund by providing information in our welcome materials to parents and including the projected revenues of the campaign in our annual budget. As our involvement in this area expands, we plan to identify other projects and programs as well as other constituents that we can draw on for future crowdfunding campaigns in an effort to deepen the engagement with our program constituents and to build a broader individual donor base beyond a relatively modest core group.

Figure 3.2. For the last fifteen years, Chabot has conducted a teen volunteer program called the Galaxy Explorers (GE). A weekly high touch program, GE enrolls 130 active high school students in free-of-charge sessions where they take classes, engage in team activities, projects and lectures.

NOTES

1. The average age of Chabot's donors is 60 and over, most gifts are $1,000 and higher.

2. See *American Dream Composite Index*, Xavier University, (2012). Accessible at http://www.americandreamcompositeindex.com/ The American Dream Composite Index™ (ADCI) is "a unique and robust measure of American sentiment that values the American Dream on a monthly basis" by encompassing behaviors, attitudes and satisfaction with economic conditions, personal well-being, societal and political institutions, cultural diversity, and the physical environment.

3. In 2014, the center had 165 adult volunteers and 130 teen volunteers in the Galaxy Explorer Program.

4. In 2012 crowdfunding campaigns lasted an average of 8.2 weeks from launch to completion. Approximately 25 percent of the goal was raised in the first 2–3.5 weeks, the last 25 percent of goal was raised in the last 2.5–3.5 weeks. See Stastista.com "The Statistics Portal." http://www.statista.com/statistics/269987/average-timeframe-of-crowdfunding-campaign-in-weeks/.

5. Devin Thorpe, "Crowdfunding for Good: Now a Growing Global Movement." Accessible at http://www.forbes.com/sites/devinthorpe/2014/01/07/crowdfunding-for-good-now-a-growing-global-movement/.

6. In 2013 a number of additional donations came in not recorded on the site but directly attributable to the campaign (some checks, and some cash). For instance, a student brought in several small donations of cash from friends and relatives in her community who preferred to give cash.

7. Mark Rovner, Pam Loeb, and Gayle Vogel, *The Next Generation of American Giving: The Charitable Habits of Generations Y, X, Baby Boomers, and Matures*. Blackbaud, August 2013, 16.

FOUR

Analysis and Interpretation

How Camp ArtyFact Solved a
Programming Problem

Mike Deetsch,[1] Toledo Museum of Art and
Greg Hardison, Kentucky Historical Society

Founded in 1836 and located in the state capitol (Frankfort), the Kentucky Historical Society (KHS) is a state agency in the Tourism, Arts, and Heritage Cabinet that collects and preserves artifacts, oral histories, and archives to share with the Commonwealth's four million plus citizens. With over 200,000 collection items, two museums, and stewardship of an 1830s Greek Revival Old State Capitol, KHS has a bounty of resources on the state's history. Since the height of the recession, however, KHS has faced difficult budget challenges along with difficulties with attendance. Of course, many museums and historical societies are facing these problems and that can be attributed to the economy, but another unique factor for KHS is its position in Frankfort. The capitol has a scant population of 25,000 but is situated approximately an hour to the east and west of Kentucky's two largest cities. The majority of Frankfort commutes in and out daily to work for the state government. This ebb and flow of population, which is centralized around a workforce, makes programming a challenge for a museum of this charge.

PLANNING

Like many museums and historical societies, the Kentucky Historical Society has begun assessing its slate of educational programming. Due to waning attendance and reduced budget allocation from state government, by the summer 2009 members of the Education Department, a group of eight full-time staff including Mike Deetsch, student programs manager, and Greg Hardison, participatory arts and programs administrator, undertook an assessment and began looking at the organization's onsite education offerings, in terms of programming type and audience as well as expenses and revenue. By winter 2010, the department also began to explore ways of attracting new audiences and developing an earned revenue model to support the newly adopted strategic plan. KHS revenue stream, prior to 2010, largely consisted of an allocation from the General Assembly, admissions revenue, membership, special events, merchandise sales, and donations to the nonprofit friends organization, the KHS Foundation. With state funds becoming more and more competitive among agencies, KHS was faced with the task of providing educational programming to its constituents on

Figure 4.1.   The educational goal for Camp ArtyFact was to be a multi-disciplinary arts and humanities program that used the KHS museum, archival, and library collections to facilitate historical thinking, improve interpretation skills, and enhance creativity in its participants.

a limited budget or be forced to find alternative means for supplementing the revenue source. Drawing upon his experiences as a museum educator at large and small institutions alike, Deetsch began to formulate ideas for a summer arts program that would utilize the collections, attract a unique audience, and generate earned income.

IMPLEMENTATION

As the Education Department began assessing its current and potential resources, Deetsch worked closely with the director of education and other student services staff, especially Hardison, to learn what programs had been previously offered, what physical resources might exist (i.e., supplies, materials, facilities) and what staff expertise we had. Deetsch learned that KHS had a long history of infusing the arts into learning experiences, most notably through its then folklife and museum theater programs. The museum theater program, directed by Hardison, also had a very significant connection with the elementary school audience, as the program had provided onsite and outreach performances to schools for over ten years. Additionally, KHS had been offering drop-in family programs like History Zone, an arts and crafts program that connected the KHS collection with a hands-on learning experience.

By February 2010, Deetsch presented a pilot program, Camp ArtyFact, to the KHS senior leadership team through the organization's project planning and review process, a proposal format used to highlight program concepts, logistics, and resources for executing and completing. Once the proposal was approved by senior leadership, dates were established and a budget and timeline were set for promotion, recruiting of participants, and hiring of contract staff. Deetsch determined that Camp ArtyFact should be set for a three-week run, because of the limited budget allocated ($7,000, beginning July 2010). Setting the camp in mid-July also allowed enough time to plan out the program, while still being able to take advantage of the summer months and school vacation. Of the initial funding, $1,000 was used for up-front costs such as marketing and supplies. The additional $6,000 would not be incurred until the camp began and would largely be spent on instructor salaries.

Camp ArtyFact intended to meet larger institutional goals including redefining KHS's approach toward developing creative and dynamic experiences for children and establishing KHS as a youth programming venue. With these goals in mind, KHS identified school-age visitors ages five to thirteen as the primary audience, specifically those that either live in Frankfort or whose parents/guardians commute to Frankfort for work. The educational goal for Camp ArtyFact was to be a multidisciplinary arts and humanities program that used the KHS museum, archival, and library collections to facilitate historical thinking, improve interpretation skills, and enhance creativity in its participants.

Deetsch also wanted to remain competitive with other summer offerings in the Frankfort area, such as the YMCA day camps, as well as be seen as a viable alternative to daycare options for working parents. In order to provide the most flexibility to our target audience (state employees), the camp was developed as a series of weeklong, half-day classes offered in both the morning and afternoon. As an incentive for parents to enroll their children for the entire day KHS provided a chaperoned lunch space free of charge.

KHS also set out a rather aggressive marketing campaign to Frankfort residents and state employees and had enough brochures printed that one could be hand delivered to every elementary and middle school student in Franklin County. Additionally, the organization was able to do direct marketing to state employees through a statewide email and paystub insert.

Deetsch determined the capacity for Camp ArtyFact was 240 students based upon a calculation of twelve classes offered during the three weeks and a maximum of twenty students per class. The goal was to enroll ninety-six students, enough to cover the costs of supplies and instructors for each of the twelve offerings. In order to reach the largest possible audience with limited staff resources, KHS used this program to initiate a new style of staff, primarily contracting freelance artists and educators to teach classes and enlisted the help of volunteers to serve as classroom assistants. This approach allowed KHS to strengthen partnerships with other state agencies, and build in-house expertise without hiring additional staff during a statewide hiring freeze. As part of this process KHS worked closely with the Kentucky Arts Council (KAC) to identify teaching artists on their Art Education Roster—a resource that connects professional artists with schools throughout the state. These instructors brought expertise as artists and art teachers, and the KHS staff provided access to collections and ways in which to engage students with the history campus.

RESULTS

By July 12, 2010, the first week of Camp ArtyFact was underway with enough students to run each class, around twelve of which would be staying for the all-day program. Overall, Camp ArtyFact successfully combined the fields of history and art to create an incredibly educational program that children had fun participating in and wanted to continue to participate in. Initial enrollment for the pilot camp session exceeded expectations, which was evident in the number of unique children enrolled (98) during the initial three-week program, the number of children who enrolled (28) in multiple classes and the evaluation results from parents and their children. In total, 140 spaces (45 percent higher than anticipated) out of 240 were filled. One initial trend indicated that membership to KHS was very low among participants: however, the majority of Camp ArtyFact participants were from Frankfort. This statistic proved to be valuable in the assessment of the program, as it demonstrated that our program had not been reaching our membership audience but had been able to connect with the local community.

Because of the initial success of Camp ArtyFact's first summer in 2010, KHS offered both fall and spring break sessions, each one week, during that fiscal year. While fall enrollment proved to be rather low, largely because not all Frankfort schools observed a fall break, the spring break camp became an instant success with the program running all four of the class offerings. Expanding on the success of 2010, by summer 2011 KHS was able to offer five weeks of Camp ArtyFact.

As a result of Camp ArtyFact's first year, KHS began to look closely at how it utilized staff and volunteers for programming. Prior to the contract staff model, KHS primarily used full and part-time staff to develop and deliver programming. With this new approach of contracting staff, full and part-time staff would remain primary program administrators: developing concept, writing catalog copy, hiring instructors, ordering supplies and materials, etc. while contract staff would be hired on an as-needed basis and be responsible for creating program content and facilitation. Additionally, volunteers began to take on a prominent role in youth programming and a new teen volunteer program was created to work specifically with Camp ArtyFact.

LESSONS LEARNED

The biggest lesson from this experience is that it is worth taking a risk on new programming as long as you can successfully manage the risk from the beginning of the process. This lesson does not mean freedom from failure, but seeks to forecast why the program will succeed or fail and how to build on that information. Will there be a loss of resource? Money? Audience? What are the potential successes that can result? New audience? New revenue model?

Another challenge faced initially, and ultimately overcome, was the limited pool of qualified contract employees. Because this was a specialty program (i.e., combining the arts and history using a museum collection), KHS had to be willing to partner with an outside organization to connect with a larger talent pool and to expand the resource base. If KHS did not have the relationship with the Kentucky Arts Council, there would not have been enough instructors to run classes during the pilot program. Once the pilot program was an established success KHS was able to attract a new pool of candidates to the program, drawing from seasoned art teachers in the region.

There were other challenges with working with qualified contract staff. After many teachers were hired, Deetsch soon discovered how uncomfortable they were teaching from the museum's collections. Either they were completely unfamiliar with the collections, or they did not know how to incorporate those collection items into their lesson planning. Because many of the contract teachers did not live in Frankfort, Deetsch and Hardison needed to find ways of making the works accessible during their planning process. Object identification was easy because many KHS collection items are available online through the KHS site, however the site lacks contextual information pertaining to those objects. Additionally, many of the teaching artists were uncomfortable teaching art through objects from a history collection: they were afraid of getting the interpretation wrong. Thus, the collection was used on a limited scale during the first year. Looking back, Deetsch should have built planning, research, and training around the use of the collections.

Another challenge during that initial summer was an understanding of how finances on the state level operated. For example, Deetsch failed to realize that contract employees could not earn more than $1,000 in a given fiscal year. As a result, some of the best instructors were unable to be hired after summer; their salaries had been maxed out for the remainder of the fiscal year after teaching a full week of camp in the summer. Another limitation was that the KHS could not exceed $1,000 in purchases from supply vendors. Again, Deetsch did not anticipate obstacles which may have been anticipated had he worked more closely with the KHS Finance Department to develop solutions for overcoming these challenges. Often with programming museum colleagues tend to collaborate only with those departments that appear to have a direct impact on said programming, such as volunteer office, curatorial or content specialists, visitor services, and marketing. Successful programming is often contingent on engaging all areas of an organization in advance—no matter their role in a project—in order to preempt any potential problems that might occur.

Figure 4.2. In summer 2014, KHS also began using t-shirts as a marketing tool. Each student that enrolled in the camp was given a t-shirt and this approach helped to instantly boost brand recognition. Moving forward, students who enroll in multiple classes will receive a t-shirt, and each week a badge will be screen printed on the back of their shirt correlating to the week of attendance.

DRILLING DOWN: WHAT'S NEXT?

Since its initial development in 2010, Camp ArtyFact has continued to evolve and thrive. The original three-week summer program has expanded to include fall and spring sessions as well as growing to five weeks in the summer. A cadre of teen volunteers are recruited and trained by the current program director, Greg Hardison.

During the summer of 2013, attendance swelled to 333 paid participants (41 percent of which were KHS members). Yielding the largest number of participants to date revealed many successes and challenges. Awareness of Camp ArtyFact has grown to the point that minimal marketing is needed (a rack card pointing to the website listing camps and enrollment procedures). In summer 2014, KHS also began using t-shirts as a marketing tool. Each student enrolled was given a t-shirt and this approach helped to instantly boost brand recognition. Moving forward, students who enroll in multiple classes will receive a t-shirt, and each week a badge will be screen printed on the back of their shirt correlating to the week of attendance.

One other major innovation took place in the summers of 2013 and 2014. The campers, teens, and interns were invited to curate an exhibition related to the program. To facilitate this, KHS collection items that connected with each of the twenty different camps were selected and placed in juxtaposition to the students' original visual and performing arts works that were displayed on the walls and through video screens. These permanent collection items were selected and interpreted through labels and simple interactives. Highlights from the exhibitions included a fashion show of clothing creations inspired by KHS textiles and clothing.

Hardison continues to experiment and find effective methods for engaging contract staff with collections. Although many collections items are viewable through online databases, there are still many items that are not as easily accessible. Hardison has also enlisted the help of other museum staff in creating virtually curated collections that can be shared with the camp instructors, so that they can plan in advance and become more comfortable with using collections in their teaching. KHS archives and collections staff have additionally selected and presented groupings of artifacts during pre-camp training days to allow contract staff time to learn about the collection and develop creative ways for incorporating those objects into their lesson plans.

Even with the above challenges, Camp ArtyFact continues to evolve and grow from the pilot program in summer 2010. As staff capacity, program format, and focus continue to take shape, Camp ArtyFact will continue to find a home in KHS programs and provide a revenue stream that serves to connect children with collections in their state's capitol.

KEY RESOURCES

Blankenship, Jody, Mike Deetsch, Stacia Kuceyseki, and Megan Wood. "Designing Education Programs that Connect Students to Collections." Technical Leaflet #254, Nashville, TN: AASLH, 2011.

National Endowment for the Arts. *How a Nation Engages with Art: Highlights from the 2012 Survey of Public Participation in the Arts.* NEA Research Report #57, September 2013.

NOTE

1. Mike Deetsch served as student programs manager at the Kentucky Historical Society before taking up the position of assistant director of education at Toledo Museum of Art in 2013. The program continues under the direction of Hardison following Deetsch's departure in spring 2013.

FIVE

"Member Plus" to "Ocean Advocate"

Rebranding a Membership Program to Support Fundraising

Nancy Enterline,
Monterey Bay Aquarium

PLANNING

Located at the ocean's edge, the world renowned Monterey Bay Aquarium is a window to the magical marine world—home to sea otters, sharks, seahorses, tuna, penguins and thousands of other marine animals. In addition to changing special exhibitions, our acclaimed permanent exhibits include a towering three-story kelp forest; touch pools and other hands-on exhibits; the award-winning Splash Zone family galleries; and the million-gallon Open Sea exhibit. Since opening thirty years ago, the aquarium has also become a leading ocean conservation organization, with global programs like our sustainable seafood initiative, Seafood Watch; ocean policy work at the state and national levels; and conservation research on threatened ocean animals like great white sharks, sea otters, and Bluefin tuna. We also provide free visits and education programs for over 100,000 schoolchildren, chaperones, and teachers each year.

Even before opening day on October 20, 1984, the aquarium created a membership program offering free admission and other benefits to its members. Enjoying steady growth over the years, the program now stands at over 75,000 households or 270,000 individuals, generating over $11 million in earned revenue annually. While a significant source of revenue on its own, the membership program also serves as the foundation of our annual fund and donor programs. From early on in the aquarium's history, we have solicited members through annual appeals and special campaigns to upgrade their support and join our donor circles, or to make an outright donation above and beyond their membership. Through this consistent effort to grow our upper levels of giving by directly appealing to members, our annual fund now generates nearly $5 million in contributed revenue each year, with members consistently representing over 90 percent of all new annual fund donors. Although a successful program—especially compared to visitor serving organization benchmarks—we share the industry challenge of finding new ways to grow and sustain our annual fund.

As is common for membership and fundraising programs, we periodically survey our members to learn more about them: their motivations for supporting the aquarium, their interests, what benefits they value most, etc. Historically, these studies typically comprised mail and phone surveys to current and lapsed members. In 2008, however, we partnered with the predictive market intelligence firm that provides data to inform the aquarium's marketing strategy to gain more sophisticated intelligence on our membership program. Notably, their methodology covers the *market* for membership, not just current members, providing real-time and actionable business intelligence as well as market potential analyses. The goals for this study included price optimization for all membership categories, evaluation of our benefit complement, and gaining psychographic and demographic information for our membership market. Using their methodology over our usual approach would allow us to align our program's pricing and offerings with a broader audience—the data would help us understand perceptions of current members about our program's pricing and offerings, but also people in the market with a high propensity for *becoming* members.

As expected, the research findings yielded important pricing data, especially to confirm that our current prices were in line with the market value for an aquarium membership across all categories. Strategic pricing is a critical part of any membership program; for the aquarium, this data helped ensure that we were optimizing earned revenue, but also creating opportunities for advancing our fundraising program. The data also answered specific questions about individual benefits that helped to inform changes in our benefit complement; we looked at perceptions of our member magazine, discounts, express entry, members' only hours, etc. to better deliver benefits that the market wanted. Most important, however, the findings revealed a significant opportunity to gain new households at our premium membership level, the "Member Plus" category, and to leverage both pricing and market attitudes to further position our membership program as a pathway to annual giving.

The data indicated that members, and people in the market who profile like members, consider the aquarium a trusted leader in ocean conservation with a high level of authority and authenticity. Furthermore, there was opportunity to reach people with a likelihood to give $250 annually (the equivalent of our "Member Plus" membership level), who considered joining the aquarium an important action for the oceans, rather than simply a transaction related to free admission and other benefits. Households at this level were *motivated by their affinity* for the aquarium and our conservation mission, rather than only the transactional value of the benefits received. The data further suggested an opportunity to grow this category of membership, including from outside of our core market, by aligning membership with a philanthropic- and mission-based proposition, rather than focusing primarily on a benefit- or value-based proposition.

As a result, we embarked on a project to rebrand our "Member Plus" category of membership to reflect the conservation ethos that was characteristic of the market for that level of giving. We changed the name from "Member Plus" to "Ocean Advocate"; established an interdepartmental team to develop a marketing plan for acquiring new members at this level; and created a new communications plan for "Ocean Advocate" members that spanned cultivation-related outreach to fundraising appeals. The expected outcome was growth in the "Ocean Advocate" category by acquiring new members, including gaining households from outside our core market; increased renewal rates from existing members at this level; an increase in upgrades to our donor levels; and increased outright gifts to the annual fund.

IMPLEMENTATION

The strategy to rebrand our $250 membership category from "Member Plus" to "Ocean Advocate" began in 2008 after receiving the initial market data and continues today as we evaluate and iterate our efforts. We commissioned the research project in the spring of 2008, received initial data in May, with final results delivered in July. We then spent the next two months developing proposed changes to the "Member Plus" category that would effectively reflect the research findings. This phase also included market testing of our proposed name change to determine what would resonate best with this "affinity-based" market of current and potential members. Discussions with senior leadership followed and the proposal was approved in October with a target implementation date of January 1, 2009. Notably, the aquarium celebrated its twenty-fifth anniversary that fall, and we felt it was important to leverage the occasion to make our program change announcement to both internal and external audiences.

Because membership is represented and promoted across multiple channels by various departments—onsite, online, in print, via staff and volunteers—the process to rollout the name change alone was extensive, yet had to be completed in a relatively short timeframe (between November 1 and December 31, 2008) to meet our deadline. In addition to audience-facing updates to signage in the aquarium and to content on the website, we implemented significant backend changes to the membership database, point of sale system, data entry procedures, and reporting;

again, all taking place before year end. We also conducted trainings for dozens of staff in multiple departments, including the entire Guest Experience frontline staff, as well as hundreds of volunteer guides. The latter was critical because staff and volunteers who interact with our nearly 2 million annual visitors are key communicators with our target audiences.

After implementing the name change, we then customized all communications to our "Ocean Advocate" members to better reflect their affinity with our conservation mission. The first step was a letter from our executive director announcing the program change. As mentioned, and reflected in the following excerpt, we leveraged the timing of the aquarium's twenty-fifth anniversary to make our announcement. We also felt it was important to express how important members themselves were to the program change; their commitment to the aquarium and conservation was the driver.

> In honor of our anniversary, as well as the vital role our members have in our institution, I am pleased to let you know that we have renamed your membership circle "Ocean Advocate" (for donors giving $250, $500, or $1,000). I hope you'll agree that this better reflects your commitment to ocean conservation.
>
> We also conducted a survey and are responding to what our members told us: that the aquarium is regarded as a trusted voice and a national leader in ocean conservation. We have achieved this stature, in great part, due to our wonderful membership that today numbers more than 70,000 households across the country.
>
> And yet, we are mindful of how much remains to be done to protect the oceans for future generations. From climate change to overfishing, the problems may seem overwhelming. But, working together, there's no limit to what we can accomplish.
>
> As an Ocean Advocate, you'll also receive more frequent email updates about critical ocean issues. If you haven't already done so, please be sure we have your current email address by contacting us at membership@mbayaq.org.
>
> Thank you for being a Monterey Bay Aquarium Ocean Advocate. I look forward to celebrating our 25th anniversary with you over the coming months.

From renewal notices to acknowledgments, we further referenced their commitment to ocean conservation and included verbiage that spoke to their membership gift as an important action for the oceans. We also increased, in volume and content, updates about our conservation programs in the email newsletter and our member magazine. This was not, however, to the detriment of visit-related messages. Members are an important visitor audience, representing between 20–25 percent of total visitation; and, our market data indicated that members who view membership as a conservation action still value their visit-related benefits. Therefore, we tied conservation messaging with the visit experience through fun and engaging stories about exhibit animals, like sea otters, that are the focus of conservation research programs, field research, and policy advocacy.

During this process, we also established an interdepartmental team to develop a marketing plan for acquiring new members at the "Ocean Advocate" level with the aim of gaining households from outside our core market. This team had representation from Membership and Development; Marketing; Online Engagement; and Conservation and Science, particularly our Seafood Watch sustainable seafood program because it already enjoyed a national reputation. We met regularly to create deliverables that included messaging, strategies, and prototypes for new benefits that could then be market tested. Our goal was to create a program that would have broad appeal to members within visiting distance, but also to those from outside our region who *might* visit. Again, because of this market's propensity to join based on their affinity with our conservation mission, we saw an opportunity to diversify the geographic reach of our program beyond a visit-centric market. This collaborative effort continued alongside the launch and implementation of our "Ocean Advocate" rebranding, but the latter was not dependent on the former.

Overall, the resources invested in the "Ocean Advocate" rebranding project were mainly staff-related: the initial implementation phase required deliverables from employees in multiple departments and input from assistant-level staff to senior leadership. Additionally, because tracking our efforts was critically important, we overhauled our data entry procedures to ensure appropriate reporting on key performance indicators over the long term. This process to analyze and update our processes for capturing membership and transactional data required a significant time investment from our database administrator and program managers in particular. The new procedures also added complexity to the data entry process, thereby adding time to our day-to-day business operations. Aside from the cost of the research that catalyzed the project, direct costs associated with the project were directed toward printing brochures (a cost we would have normally incurred that time of year, so not considered new spending) and the initial mailing to members and donors. Ongoing additional costs resulted from creating more granular segments in our monthly renewal mailings and sending additional communications to "Ocean Advocate" members outside of our typical cultivation efforts. Where possible, however, we leveraged email and digital channels to create cost savings.

Although seemingly a simple aspect of this project, the move to rename our $250 membership category from "Member Plus" to "Ocean Advocate" was not without challenges. The name "Member Plus" had been in place since the category's inception in 1994 and there was some initial resistance to making the change, especially from longtime staff and volunteers. Other colleagues were skeptical about the research findings and questioned the origin or appropriateness of the new name. As a result, we added more details from the research to our staff and volunteer presentations, including how we tested the "Ocean Advocate" name with our current members and the general membership market. We also emphasized that the program changes were ultimately driven by current members and prospective members, and stressed how this new strategy would further bolster support for the aquarium and our conservation programs in both the near and longer term.

Logistically, the timeframe we allotted for the name change was challenging: six weeks from finalizing the plan to implementation on January 1. However, providing stakeholders with the background information and research data as previously described helped galvanize support for

Table 5.1   Project Timeline 2008–2010

Research Project	Comprehensive pricing and benefits study with market research firm	3 months
Developed Program	Finalized membership category name; developed comprehensive implementation plan	3 months
Implemented Program Changes	Revised database and point of sale systems; updated procedures; updated print materials, website, and signage	(November 2008–January 2009)
Training	Presentations to staff and volunteers across multiple departments	December 2008–January 2009
Initial Communication	Letter from executive director to introduce new name and highlight connection between membership and our conservation work	January 2009
Ongoing Communications	Segmented renewals, acknowledgments, fundraising appeals, etc. to better reflect affinity with conservation mission	January 2009–ongoing
Updated Processes and Procedures	Updated data entry processes and procedures to ensure thorough tracking and reporting	January 2009
National Marketing Effort	Interdepartmental team worked on strategies to gain new households from outside our core market	January 2009–2010
Evaluation	Tracking and comparing key performance indicators	Mid-2010 to present

meeting the deliverable requirements. People also understood and agreed with the strategy to align the program change with our twenty-fifth anniversary. Finally, the stretch goal of broadening our base of supporters at the $250 level from outside our core visitor market was negatively impacted by the Great Recession, which began shortly after we launched the "Ocean Advocate" rebranding. As a result, we did not launch a substantive effort to gain new members from outside of California as part of this initiative.

RESULTS

To evaluate our efforts, we analyzed acquisition and renewal transaction numbers, revenue, and the number of upgrades to higher levels of annual giving from the "Ocean Advocate" audience. Evaluation began in earnest in mid-2010, after we completed our year end fundraising campaign in 2009, and after gaining enough transactions from acquisition and ongoing renewals in the year following the program change. Although our transactional and household number results fluctuated slightly in the years since we launched the "Ocean Advocate" membership category, and we had to forego a national marketing effort, the program has overall met its original objectives. This is especially true when looking at revenue growth and the numbers of upgrades to higher levels of giving. The key performance indicators from 2008 to 2013 are reflected in table 5.2. It is useful to note that we raised the Ocean Advocate level rate to $275 in 2013, which contributed to the increase in revenue that year.

Although we encountered some aforementioned skepticism when launching this program, the results really speak for themselves, and it has since been very well received by staff and volunteers throughout the Aquarium. In particular, the Guest Experience team and others who communicate directly with our members and guests appreciate that the name "Ocean Advocate" provides an immediate talking point to connect membership giving with our conservation mission. Additionally, continued market testing has reinforced the affinity that members giving at this level have with our mission. Again, this affinity does not preclude these members from valuing visit-related benefits such as free admission or express entry; it means that they are more likely to view their membership payment as an important action for the oceans than members at lower levels who place a higher premium on the transactional benefits of their membership. By speaking to "Ocean Advocate" members as just that, advocates for the ocean, we are better able to appeal to their commitment to ocean conservation and the trust they place in the Monterey Bay Aquarium to do good work on behalf of the oceans. This shift in emphasis, even

Table 5.2. Results

	2008	2009	2010	2011	2012	2013
Total Households	17,344	16,971	18,454	19,619	22,361	25,399
Upgrades to Donor Levels	201	128	238	203	321	314
Retention Rate	78%	85%	95%	92%	93%	90%
Revenue	$3,841,739	$3,874,638	$4,256,811	$4,415,847	$4,941,692	$5,609,041

if a seemingly simple shift in hindsight, has greatly contributed to growth in that membership level and to higher levels of giving from this audience.

LESSONS LEARNED

Leveraging a membership program to create a strong annual fund is, of course, not unique to the Monterey Bay Aquarium—although it can be challenging for organizations where the membership program is not under the umbrella of development. Moreover, conducting research for program evaluation or to gain insights about audiences is not unique to us. However, many organizations undertake audience research in departmental silos, gaining data about a particular audience in a vacuum. This project represented the first time we conducted a robust study for *membership* using the more sophisticated approach and broader audience that has helped make our organization's *marketing* efforts so successful. Many nonprofits struggle with silos within their organization, and some of those silos prevent organizations from asking members to become donors, or to leverage the best practices of marketing and market research to better support efforts like fundraising. In our connected world where members and donors choose how and when to engage with us, especially through social media channels, we are doing a great disservice to ourselves by operating in outdated silos. As nonprofit marketing thought leader Colleen Dilenschneider reflects, "a lack of collaboration between development/fundraising and marketing/communications comes at perhaps one of the most extreme expenses for a nonprofit organization."[1] As indicated, this project's success also hinged on engaging work groups from Guest Experience, our volunteer program and online engagement, among others. As such, one of the most significant positive outcomes of this project was building true collaboration across multiple stakeholders where, at times, tension previously existed. These collaborations have since grown and expanded into other areas since 2009, especially in the areas of online engagement and enhancing onsite visibility for membership and fundraising.

Market research can, of course, be prohibitively expensive for many nonprofits. Yet, understanding the attitudes and perceptions of members and prospective members is invaluable when strategizing opportunities for growth and retention, and to evaluate spending on benefits fulfillment and other stewardship efforts. Even if predictive market research is out of reach for an organization, it is critically important to find ways to solicit feedback from members: how your supporters perceive the membership program, and the organization more broadly, yields important insights that can increase revenues and identify areas for cost savings. It is also critical to engage members in philanthropy—as our research indicated, some already consider their membership payment a contribution and there are likely opportunities to leverage that affinity to generate more philanthropic support from members. Lastly, having market data to inform membership pricing has created better alignment with general admission pricing, greatly alleviating any potential concern about membership "competing" with ticket sales. More relevant to this project, however, this data-informed pricing strategy has significantly contributed to the growth in our premium "Ocean Advocate" category because the price truly reflects market demand.

DRILLING DOWN: WHAT'S NEXT?

Given the overall success of the "Ocean Advocate" project—including the individual elements discussed such as pricing optimization, communications segmentation, and fundraising strategies—we plan to continue the program in much of its current form. We continue to make adjustments based on metrics; for instance, we no longer segment all communications to Ocean Advocate members, preferring to utilize segmentation where it has yielded the greatest results. As is prudent for any membership and donor program, we are increasingly focused on retention efforts for our new Ocean Advocate members and those who upgraded from Ocean Advocate into higher levels of annual support. Indeed, with 50 percent growth in the five years since we launched the program, we are mindful that retention is one of our greatest challenges for sustaining the program. When considering how we can build upon the project, we continue to evaluate strategies for engaging new members from outside of our core market; although the economy's slow recovery has continued to render this goal less plausible than before the Great Recession. Even so, we currently have members in all fifty states and thirty-two different countries. As our conservation programs continue to gain prominence on the national and even international stage, we anticipate more opportunities to grow philanthropic support from audiences, regardless of where they live, who have an affinity for our conservation work and a propensity to become "Ocean Advocate" members of the Monterey Bay Aquarium.

NOTE

1. Colleen Dilenschneider, "6 Strategic Reasons for Membership Teams to Be Involved with Social Media," *Know Your Own Bone* (blog), November 10, 2014, http://colleendilen.com/2014/08/20/6-strategic-reasons-for-membership-teams-to-be-involved-with-social-media/.

Six

Check It Out!

A Case Study of the New Children's Museum's Program of Circulating Membership Cards in Public Libraries

Karen Coutts, Independent Consultant and Former Director of Development for the New Children's Museum

An innovative and collaborative approach can be the ideal solution for a museum looking to make its mark in a resource-scarce industry. Such was the case for the New Children's Museum when it opened to the public in 2008. This newly constructed contemporary facility provided 50,000 square feet of space in downtown San Diego and pioneered a model for audience engagement. Integrating features from both art museums and children's museums, the New Children's Museum (NCM) brought these elements together to create something new: an organization focused on participatory contemporary art for families.

As has been the case since its opening, every artwork in the New Children's Museum is created by a living artist, encourages participation, and is designed with children in mind. The mainstay of NCM's model for engagement is that it transforms itself in alternating years. This is achieved through the creation of an original themed exhibition which fills all three floors of the museum. On view for eighteen months, the museum then shutters for four weeks while the old exhibition is removed and a wholly new one installed. These original exhibitions are the fulcrum of NCM's innovative approach and are based on the philosophy of Allan Kaprow. Best known as the father of "happenings" and an artist who made his mark by blurring the lines between art and life, Kaprow's ideology lives on at the New Children's Museum.

Permanent studio spaces that transition between indoor and outdoor areas were integral to the contemporary green-designed building by architect Rob Wellington Quigley. These open spaces allow kids to create free-form artworks from clay, paint, and recycled objects. Access to art supplies and opportunities for unstructured play are also critical components to

NCM's new model of engagement. The studio spaces are fully staffed and provide multiple occasions for children to create projects that can be left for display or taken home.

PLANNING

In November 2007, six months prior to the public opening, the team at the New Children's Museum was still in the process of working on how to most effectively present this new concept to funders and the public. The staff focused on achieving the mission: to stimulate imagination, creativity, and critical thinking in children and families through inventive and engaging experiences with contemporary art.

The leadership team faced the same challenges as any new museum: attracting audiences, gaining support, and building membership. Because the New Children's Museum was such a different concept, there was an added challenge of communicating this to an audience for whom there was no context. Using a collaborative approach the team at NCM found solutions that could address issues faced by multiple departments.

One project that was emblematic of the multi-layered solution was "Check Out the New Children's Museum." Still going strong, this program was introduced to provide circulating membership cards in public libraries throughout San Diego. This novel approach allows each card to be checked out, like a book or video. During the loan period, the family receives all the benefits of museum membership. The purpose of the program was to:

- Raise awareness for a new museum in the community
- Offer free access to families without the ability to pay admission
- Provide an opportunity for families to sample the museum before becoming members
- Fund operating needs through outside donations

Launched six months after the opening of the museum, "Check Out the New Children's Museum" has been incredibly successful and remains a mainstay of NCM's access programs in 2015.

IMPLEMENTATION

From original concept through program launch, "Check Out the New Children's Museum" took six months. What follows is the progression from the idea through implementation, as well as results and plans for the future. The concept of "Check Out the New Children's Museum" began

May–July 2008: Identified issues facing each department: Development, Membership, Marketing, Visitor Services

July 2008: Conceptualized a program that served cross-departmental needs: "Check Out the New Children's Museum"

August–September 2008: Met with city library staff to determine interest and fit within traditional parameters for libraries

August 2008: Began fundraising campaign to underwrite circulating memberships

October 2008: Created entries in NCM and library databases representing each library branch card

October 2008: Developed membership incentives for "try it then buy it" membership model

November 2008: Designed, printed, and distributed circulating membership cards to thirty-two branch libraries

November 2008: Promoted awareness of program with press release and in-branch marketing posters

with three important ideas. First, there was a need to encourage families of all economic means to visit the museum. Next, operating funds were required to cover costs to run the museum. Finally, the museum needed to generate overall awareness of the organization and its offerings. Collaborative discussions led to the idea that circulating membership cards could serve all these purposes. The cards would be publically available through the library, and would provide users with benefits of membership including free admission, discounts on parking, and ticket purchases as well as at the café and gift shop.

A relationship with the San Diego City Libraries was essential for the success of the project. The partnership began with meetings between NCM staff and members from the San Diego City Library to define logistics. It was determined that NCM's cards could be placed into the same system as books and videos, and therefore could circulate to anyone with a library card. In an effort to serve as many guests as possible, cards were placed into the same cycle as videos. This provided families with ten days of use of the circulating membership card.

NCM staff suspected there would be two types of program consumers: those who used the cards because they could not afford admission; and those with ability who were looking for a chance to sample the museum before making a financial commitment. For the second group, the goal was to provide a "try it then buy it" model that would convince them to purchase their own membership. For those without funds to pay for admission, the program would emerge as a cornerstone of NCM's community access initiative while serving as an attractive program for funders to support.

Figure 6.1. Image of "Check Out the New Children's Museum" circulating membership card.

One major strength of "Check Out" was that nearly all of its costs were standard operating expenses for the museum. Naturally at launch there were additional costs including design and printing of the cards, program promotion, input to a donor database, and general program management. However, the bulk of day-to-day costs for the program were part of the museum's operating budget. The New Children's Museum is hands-on, consequently daily expenses include some significant hard costs. Thousands of gallons of paint and hundreds of pounds of clay are used each year in the studios, and are augmented by an array of additional supplies—from fabric, glue, and chalk to pipe cleaners and glitter. All of NCM's studios are part of the daily museum experience and are staffed by Visitor Services team members whose engagement is critical. Funders were approached with a specific request that showed the museum's cost per child for a standard day spent in the museum (staff time + supplies used). This cost, multiplied by the number of people expected to use the membership cards each year, resulted in a concrete cost to undertake the program on a day-to-day basis.

Funders appreciated the opportunity to underwrite a program that allowed access for families of all income levels to visit the museum. The New Children's Museum received funds from several groups including local, regional, and national funders. While some government and foundation support was received, corporate funding was particularly robust. Ford Motor Company, Qualcomm, and CarMax were the initial funders of this program, providing $52,000 toward its launch.

Once the concept for "Check Out" was fully developed, a card was designed that would be small enough to transport, durable enough to withstand circulation, and large enough not to easily be misplaced. The final design was a folded 5"x5" heavily laminated card that included a description of the program, the museum's physical and electronic addresses, a list of membership benefits, as well as logo recognition for funders.

For fundraising and reporting purposes, it was essential that NCM be able to track use of the cards. Using the donor database Raiser's Edge, individual records were created for each library branch and a scannable membership number was affixed to the outside of each card. Every time the card was presented, it could be scanned as would a traditional membership card. This allowed NCM to collect data on the number of times each circulating membership card was used. After NCM completed this step, cards were sent to the San Diego Central Library. There, each card received a bar code and was entered into their circulation system. Finally, cards were distributed to each city branch library for public use. Staff librarians recommended the cards not be shelved, but instead be held behind the circulation desks. A joint effort between libraries and NCM ensured that damaged or lost cards were replaced with fresh ones.

In order to promote "Check Out the New Children's Museum," NCM created a joint press release with the library and corporate funders to highlight the program. This coordinated effort—that went to press November 4, 2008—maximized the number of news outlets that received the press release. As a result, a prominent article appeared in San Diego's largest newspaper, the *San Diego Union Tribune*. Over the course of the next month, articles about "Check Out" appeared in more than a dozen publications. In addition to press coverage, laminated posters were designed, printed, and distributed to every library branch to promote the program and recognize funders.

One of the great advantages of the "Check Out" program was that the resources required to undertake it were minimal. Most of those resources can be measured in hours rather than dollars. Once the concept was developed, the program included meetings between library staff and NCM's marketing, visitor services, and membership representatives (three–four hours).

Funding proposals were created and submitted by the development team (eight–twelve hours), while donor relationships were created and sponsor benefits solidified (6–8 hours). The membership staff was responsible for entering data into Raiser's Edge (2–3 hours). The marketing team created, distributed, and coordinated the press release between NCM, the library, and funders (6–7 hours), and they designed and printed the cards and posters (6–8 hours). No outside consultants were hired for the project, and total hard costs to launch it were under $3,000 (for printing). Ongoing management remains minimal in the form of reporting and card replacement (1 hour per week), stewardship of existing funders and creation of proposals to support the program (4–5 hours per month).

RESULTS

"Check Out the New Children's Museum" quickly became popular, drawing families of all kinds to the museum. As the launch was just before the winter holidays, it drew families on break. A strong community engagement tool, it has consistently allowed families to explore the museum on their own terms, on a day and at a time that works within their schedule. This acts as a complement to a monthly Free Sunday, underwritten by Target, which welcomes thousands of families on the second Sunday of the month for a free experience.

"Check Out the New Children's Museum" exceeded all expectations. At the onset, the demand for this program was an unknown. NCM aimed for two cards to be made available in each city branch library. As quickly as the program was announced, it was widely embraced by the community and all cards were checked out. The average wait for a family to receive a card has been approximately three weeks.

The success of the San Diego City Library program prompted a phone call from the San Diego County Libraries. They approached NCM to ask if the program could be replicated in all of their thirty-six branches. This was undertaken, with the same positive results. Two cards were provided to each county branch library. Since the program's launch in 2008, all 136 cards have been checked out every single day of the year.

Beyond strict use of the cards, it is worth noting the impact that this program has had on membership. For those who had the means to become members, "Check Out" was the perfect introduction to the benefits they could enjoy all year. NCM began offering a discount to those using the "Check Out" card to purchase membership. By the end of NCM's first year the museum proudly boasted a membership base of 7,500 families—approximately 8 percent of whom came to the museum through the "Check Out" program.

LESSONS LEARNED

One of the data points that would have been useful to leverage, but ultimately was not, was a tracking of card usage by neighborhood. This information would have been useful in two ways. First, it would allow for supplementary cards to be provided branches in low-income neighborhoods with high use. Second, if higher-income neighborhoods were clearly aware of the "try it then buy it" model, those neighborhoods could be targeted by zip code in membership acquisition mailings.

Unfortunately, data was unable to be tracked as hoped. The membership cards circulate like videos which means if an individual wants to check out a card from their local branch, and it isn't available, that person is placed on a waiting list for the next available card. When a card becomes available (regardless of the card's home branch), it is then sent to the branch where the patron has requested it. Because cards follow the patron and move from branch to branch, neighborhood data was not useful. NCM had not considered this issue at the onset of the program.

After realizing the ways in which the cards were being used, a suggestion was made that cards be locked to individual branches. After much deliberation, the decision was made to keep the existing model due to the belief that a greater number of overall families would have the opportunity to experience the museum through wide circulation of cards. Thus visitor-use trumped the need to track data. Nevertheless, future iterations of this program might weigh these two options and consider incorporating user data as well as borrowing protocols.

DRILLING DOWN: WHAT'S NEXT?

Success of this program has been measured in a number of ways—how often cards are used, diversity of families using them, financial support for the program, and overall museum awareness. However, no measurement of the program's success is stronger than the fact that it has been replicated. The San Diego Museum of Art, the Reuben H. Fleet Science Center, and the San Diego Museum of Man adopted the same program using the model created by NCM. The public branch libraries continue to be enamored by these programs and several have signs promoting all the circulating membership cards they offer.

One hope for the future of this program is to introduce "Check Out" into the public school system. The goal would be to provide low-income schools with circulating membership cards that could be held by the school librarian. Similar to the public library model, the plan would be to have a student check out the card, use it for ten days, then return it to the school library for others to use. NCM had begun researching this but was deterred by an obstacle that remains challenging to overcome. Due to budget cuts, many public schools no longer have a librarian; and those that do have a librarian face restricted hours and programming such that there is no additional time available to manage special programs. For the "Check Out" program to work on a consistent basis, a librarian or other school staff member must be willing to manage the circulating cards. School administrations and PTAs have also been approached to manage the program, but no one has yet successfully taken it on. Successful management of the program would require someone who could manage the card check out process, track down cards that are not returned, and act as a liaison between the school and the New Children's Museum.

Prior to the launch of the program, concerns were voiced that "Check Out" might not be tenable because of possible revenue cannibalization. These concerns proved unfounded. Meanwhile the excellent press coverage, goodwill from the community, outside support from funders, and the ability to provide access to low-income families have proven the program a success.

Staying true to the roots inspired by artist Allan Kaprow, the New Children's Museum is pleased to be a place that encourages participation by diverse audiences. "Check Out" has proven an important tool toward this end. The New Children's Museum is proud of the "Check Out" program and sincerely hopes that other museums across the country will adopt it in an effort to broaden access, expand their reach, and enrich their communities. Further, the program's appeal to donors, and its ability to attract new members makes financial sense for an institution to consider.

KEY RESOURCES

County of San Diego. "Check Out a Free Pass to the New Children's Museum at the County Library." http://www.sdcl.org/pr_2012-12-12.html.

San Diego Public Library. "Special Resources." http://www.sandiego.gov/public-library/services/specialresources/.

The New Children's Museum. www.thinkplaycreate.org.

Seven

Leveraging the Public-Private Partnership to Transform an Abandoned, Elevated Railway into New York City's Most Exciting Public Amenity

Vicky U. Lee, Friends of the High Line

Today, the High Line is one of New York City's best-loved destinations, with annual visitation that far surpasses that of long-established landmarks such as the Empire State Building, the Museum of Modern Art, and the Statue of Liberty. Behind this internationally acclaimed model of innovative adaptive reuse is the tremendous story of two strangers, Joshua David and Robert Hammond—wholly inexperienced in urban planning, historic preservation, landscape architecture, or really any field one might associate with the High Line today—who successfully built a coalition of private and public support that saved an abandoned, historic, industrial rail structure from demolition and transformed it into a 1.5-mile long, thoughtfully designed, lushly planted, and meticulously maintained public park, thirty feet above street level, free and open to the public 365 days per year.

The public-private partnership behind the High Line is comprised of the City of New York and its Department of Parks and Recreation, which owns the physical structure itself, and Friends of the High Line—the private, nonprofit organization with 501(c)3 status founded in 1999 by David and Hammond that successfully advocated for its preservation and that, via a license agreement with the City and the Parks Department, runs the day-to-day maintenance, operations, and programming of the High Line. Every gardener, custodian, park ranger, and maintenance technician on the High Line is an employee of Friends of the High Line (Friends). Every work of art presented by High Line Art and the 400+ public programs on the High Line are curated by Friends to engage the millions of visitors who walk the High Line each year.[1]

Even as quickly as the High Line has been accepted as an icon of the New York City landscape, the path to bringing this unique amenity to the public was replete with challenges.

PLANNING

The High Line was designed by the team of James Corner Field Operations, Diller Scofidio + Renfro, and Piet Oudolf. Its construction proceeded in phases, with each section roughly half a mile in length: Section 1 broke ground in April 2006, and opened to the public in June 2009; work continued to build Section 2 without interruption for it to be opened to the public in June 2011; the groundbreaking of the third and northernmost section of the High Line, known as the High Line at the Rail Yards, took place in September 2012, with Phase 1 of the Rail Yards opened to the public in September 2014.[2]

Though it may be hard to believe now, when David and Hammond first formed Friends of the High Line back in 1999, they faced endless questions and obstacles. Would the property stakeholders ever agree to support this vision to build a park on an elevated train trestle? And if so, would it need structural repairs? Asbestos abatement? Lead paint removal? Beyond the basics of structural soundness and public safety, there was the question of design. What should the new High Line look like? How could this structure be reimagined to make the most of what

Figure 7.1. Aerial view of the High Line.

remained of it? Who would create the concept? Who would have to approve the design concept? And lurking behind all of those questions remained yet another crucial component: funding. How much would all of this cost? Who would pay for it? And how?

Such questions plague any new project, whether it's a commercial start-up or a nonprofit. Even well established organizations may face them when tackling a new kind of initiative. For Friends, balancing a public-private partnership seemed to be not only the right path to choose but *the only path* to advancing their vision with great success.

Similar to the governance structure of the High Line today, the construction of the High Line was also a result of the successful public-private partnership between Friends and the City of New York. At various points in the High Line's rebirth as a public park, Friends relied on funding from both the private and public sectors. This course of action, however, did not start with great strategic planning, but with one methodical tactic following another that eventually revealed a proven fundraising strategy. Friends continually leveraged one side of support to inspire the other to fuel the High Line's forward progress, and skillfully navigating this relationship remains a key factor in Friends' fundraising success to date.

IMPLEMENTATION

In the early days of advocacy, small gifts from private individuals and foundations powered Friends of the High Line's efforts, eventually giving them the tools to make their case to the New York City Council and its then-speaker, Gifford Miller, and then-Mayor Michael Bloomberg, leveraging less than $200,000 in private philanthropic gifts to secure over $43 million in public funding from the City of New York for capital construction and working with CSX Transportation, Inc., the private railroad company that owned the disused structure to accept what came to be known as Sections 1 and 2 of the High Line as public land belonging to the City of New York.

In turn, this public capital funding allowed for detailed design work to move forward, which gave Friends the visual materials to share their vision with the world—the world of prospective private donors. Knowing that the City of New York was not only lending moral support to the High Line, but also financial support, made the project that much more real—and that much more feasible—to all who learned of Friends' plans. The public funds committed by the City of New York helped leverage private funds, with Donald Pels, the great mobile technology pioneer, media executive, and philanthropist, writing the very first check for $1 million to support capital construction. Soon after, media mogul Barry Diller and

---

Project Timeline

1999: Friends of the High Line incorporates as a 501(c)3, acknowledging that the City of New York was not going to preserve the High Line without private intervention

1999–2003: Friends raises contributions from private individuals and foundations to build the case to the City

2003–2004: New York City Council and the Office of the Mayor commit $43 million in capital construction allocations to the High Line

2005: CSX Transportation, Inc. donates the physical structure to the City of New York. Friends leverages public funding to secure first major private gifts and officially launch the first Campaign for the High Line; other public funding from city, state, and federal government budgets is allocated to the project

2006: Construction breaks ground on the High Line

2009: Section 1 of the High Line opens to the public

2011: Section 2 of the High Line opens to the public

City of New York tells Friends that no more public capital funding will be directed to the High Line

Friends acquires and announces a special Rail Yards challenge grant to jump-start the new campaign for the High Line at the Rail Yards; hires a dedicated campaign manager to focus on private campaign contributions

2014: High Line at the Rail Yards opens to the public

---

fashion designer Diane von Furstenberg announced a $5 million commitment from the Diller–von Furstenberg Family Foundation to the project, helping Friends launch the Campaign for the High Line to raise a total of $50 million in private philanthropic support toward capital construction and an endowment for the long-term financial security of the High Line. The City of New York also leaned its zoning and negotiating powers to the High Line to help secure nearly $7 million in real estate development-related contributions to the project.

All of these funds, and more from the City, New York State, and U.S. governments, built the first two sections of the High Line, with the City of New York providing more than two-thirds of the total cost of building Sections 1 and 2. A clear relationship had appeared between public and private support. Moreover, Friends saw evidence of how one commitment could spur another.

As the second phase of construction neared completion, the City made it clear to Friends that it felt its financial obligation to the High Line had been met and that Friends should not anticipate any future capital allocations for the remaining northernmost third of the High Line, known as the High Line at the Rail Yards. Friends launched a new phase of the

Campaign for the High Line with renewed focus on private philanthropic support, beginning with a two-pronged strategy: return to the most committed donors who had supported the first campaign and simultaneously engage them in efforts to cultivate new donors to preserve, design, build, and open the High Line at the Rail Yards to the public. Friends also continued to cultivate the City relationship in the hope that there might still be some allocations to be set aside for the High Line when budget time came.

This approach, in some ways, was a déjà-vu moment. The High Line at the Rail Yards was still private property, owned by CSX Transportation, Inc., and the fate of that final half-mile stretch of the structure was far from certain. The storied site had seen many proposals come and go, and the lion's share suggested tearing some or all of the High Line down in that area. There was a simultaneous push on the advocacy side and the fundraising side to bring the High Line at the Rail Yards to fruition. As efforts on the advocacy side focused on the same zoning law changes and community input forums that had helped secure the first two sections of the High Line for its transformation into a public park, the fundraising side was looking to grow its resources to properly prepare for the considerable new goal ahead, with the knowledge that the City of New York was not going to write a check.

Without a significant public allocation for the Rail Yards section, Friends focused on securing a significant private gift to energize the announcement of its second campaign, and they found it in the Tiffany & Co. Foundation, who announced a challenge grant of $5 million at the opening of Section 2 of the High Line. As seen previously, Friends was able to leverage this challenge grant in solicitation meetings, ultimately securing a new $5 million gift from Don Pels and an extraordinary $20 million grant from the Diller-von Furstenberg Family Foundation.

This announcement was shortly followed by the hiring of a full-time, dedicated campaign staff person. This was a change in approach: in its first phase of the campaign, Friends had relied largely on fundraising consultants. Entering its second phase, with a much larger fundraising goal than the first, the need for a campaign manager was clear. In December 2011, I was hired as director, Campaign for the High Line. Additionally, because it was perceived as the top priority by both co-founders, the campaign also received the respect and attention of nearly anyone on staff when requested.

Another important resource needed to meet the campaign goal was a strong pipeline management system. Like many nonprofit organizations, Friends keeps its donor database in Raiser's Edge (RE). While Friends undertook the long and arduous task of bringing the entire development team's pipeline management systems into RE under the Prospect module, I compiled all the relevant campaign information that came across my desk into an Excel spreadsheet, which became my daily tracking document.[3]

Friends also engaged professional data aggregators such as WealthEngine and Relationship Science (RelSci) to aid in prospect research. Reliable in-house reports on capacity and philanthropic preferences, pulled together with these resources, have proven helpful in understanding a prospective donor's philanthropic priorities and interests, as well as the appropriate level of giving to request, if the giving history aligned with any of the work of Friends.

Utilizing data and research, a standard campaign presentation, as well as a standard solicitation script to help guide the solicitor were prepared. The scripts are tailored to each prospect to ensure that the solicitor would be focusing on what the organization knew to interest the prospective donor. The script also helps the solicitor pace the meeting, ensuring the ask is made before the appointment was over. Clear financial tracking—understanding how much cash Friends needed for capital construction and when—was also an essential piece of the puzzle, helping to define Friends' urgent message.

Friends also made a design decision to fully develop only the eastern half of the Rail Yards section in the first phase of construction and leave the western half largely untouched—overrun by a wild, self-seeded landscape—with the addition of a simple walking path, to be known as the Interim Walkway.[4] By simplifying the design scope of the western Rail Yards, Friends was able to maintain a capital budget for this phase of work that could be supported by a campaign goal that included more endowment funding as well to total $130 million.

Although this goal felt aspirational, it also felt attainable, especially with the knowledge that, through zoning regulations, the City was working to help secure nearly $30 million in construction funding from the developers of the Rail Yards site for the High Line at the Rail Yards' construction. Friends continued its advocacy to ultimately save the entire Rail Yards section of the High Line from demolition by convincing the various stakeholders to choose a development plan for that area that preserved the entire High Line as it stood.

With the script, presentation, financials, and a research profile, Friends pursued every past donor, every prospective donor, and sometimes even donors who were currently paying out their pledged commitments—asking everyone to make a meaningful gift that would count.

Friends continued to demonstrate great fundraising success and made its case to the City for additional public capital funds to help close a cash flow gap and maintain the construction schedule for the High Line at the Rail Yards. These efforts resulted in $11 million in new public funds, half from the New York City Council under the leadership of Speaker Christine Quinn, and half from Mayor Bloomberg, over the course of this phase of the campaign. Despite earlier indications to the contrary, these public allocations were motivated as much by Friends' success raising private funds as a desire by those public officials who had started this project wishing to fulfill that legacy. All of these resources and strategies empowered a very small team of our co-founders, vice president of development, myself, and the occasional support of other colleagues, to raise the funds needed to design, build, and open the first phase of the High Line at the Rail Yards to the public under budget and on schedule in 2014.

RESULTS

Friends of the High Line worked to build on each small success to achieve the next loftier goal, always aspiring to greater inspirational heights and looking to leverage one funding commitment into the next funding commitment on both sides of the public-private partnership. This strategy built the first two sections of the High Line and laid the path for the northernmost section of this historical structure, known as the High Line at the Rail Yards.

On September 20, 2014, Friends, along with seven hundred of its closest supporters, volunteers, and community members, cut the ribbon on the High Line at the Rail Yards. Because the campaign was able to meet its cash goals each year and keep construction within budget, Friends finally achieved its original mission to preserve, transform, and open to the public the entire High Line from Gansevoort Street to 34th Street. Every measure of the campaign's success can be seen in this new section of the park, which received a uniformly positive reception from the public and in the press.

LESSONS LEARNED

When beginning a new project or initiative, finding the seed funding necessary can seem unbearably daunting. But Friends' co-founders held a profound belief in their mission and its benefits for New York City and made every effort to convince everyone they met of the same—and then strategically leveraged each relationship and eventually each financial commitment to bring in more and more.

In the beginning, Friends focused on the private funds immediately available, looking to friends and friends of friends of David and Hammond. That network grew as the profile of their dream to reimagine the High Line grew, eventually bringing in enough funding to make a serious, data-driven, economic argument to the City of New York, which in turn led to significant public funding. Public funding gave Friends' mission legitimacy to make the case to private individuals, corporations, and foundations that their support of the High Line would bring something spectacular to New York City's cultural landscape. And the success in raising private funds continued to bring public funding even after the City of New York indicated that no more would be allocated to the High Line.

The campaign experience of Friends shows that belief in the mission is paramount, as that will provide the motivation needed to ask again, and again, and again. It will provide the strength to smile when you're told no, to turn around and ask someone new after you're told no, and not to be discouraged by others' unwillingness to support your mission. Add openness to identify opportunities, agility to respond quickly to them, and perseverance to see the mission through, and you will be able to build on each success—and even on failures—to leap to the next opportunity.

DRILLING DOWN: WHAT'S NEXT?

Despite the successes of the campaign to date, Friends of the High Line remains aware that this model is most successful when applied for a finite period of time. The nature of any campaign is defined as being a focused effort to accomplish a specified goal within a limited timeframe. There is no doubt that there was a risk in moving directly from completing a $50 million campaign into starting a new $130 million campaign without pause. It puts strain on the organization's donors, but also on the organization itself—on its staff and its leadership. There are also drawbacks to highly visible success, as it can undermine an organization's need message; though, on the other hand, donors are often also drawn to successful projects.

Even so, every lesson learned in this process is being applied to the philanthropic fundraising efforts for our annual operations, which will always be the bulk source of revenue for Friends. What Friends witnessed over and over again was that each financial commitment secured for the campaign was exponentially more powerful for its ability to help secure the following financial commitment, and the same can be said of transitioning campaign donors to annual operations support. This transition is of the utmost importance for the long-term financial security of the organization. On the public side, political changes like a new mayor, speaker of the New York City Council, and Parks commissioner have all drastically changed the public funding allocations, and future administration changes are a built-in unknown for the foreseeable future.

And, of course, there remains the question of one final capital construction effort in the future, once the western Rail Yards area—currently existing as the Interim Walkway—is ready for redesign and construction. While the organization does not feel ready to take this initiative on in the immediate future, it will eventually be necessary to perform the same structural repairs on the western Rail Yards that were executed on the rest of the High Line, at which point, having maintained those donor relationships in the interim, Friends will have to re-engage this very special group of high capacity donors with the "build" mission once more. It is difficult to predict what the messaging around that future campaign will be, or whether that campaign will see a combination of public and private funding—but factors for consideration include the City administration at that time, public opinion of the High Line, and the economic health of New York City, among many others. But as long as the public-private partnership established for the daily operation of the High Line is maintained, this relationship will always be relevant to the High Line's health and success.

KEY RESOURCES

Bay Area Economics. *High Line Revenue Generation Study*. San Francisco: Bay Area Economics, 2007.

Cohen, Steven. "The Highline: Public-Private Partnership and Bloomberg's Leadership Creates a Great New Park." *Huffington Post*, May 31, 2011.

David, Joshua. *Reclaiming the High Line: A Project of the Design Trust for Public Space with Friends of the High Line*. New York: Design Trust for Public Space, 2002.

David, Joshua, and Robert Hammond. *High Line: The Inside Story of New York City's Park in the Sky*. New York: Farrar, Straus and Giroux, 2011.

Davidson, Justin. "Where the High Line Ends." *New York*, March 14, 2012.

Foderaro, Lisa W. "Record $20 Million Gift to Help Finish the High Line Park." *New York Times*, October 26, 2011.

Friends of the High Line. "Friends of the High Line." https://www.thehighline.org/.

Goldberger, Paul. "The Final Segment of the High Line Is Stunningly Refreshing." *Vanity Fair*, September 22, 2014. http://www.vanityfair.com/online/daily/2014/09/high-line-final-segment-new-york.

Harris, Jeffrey A. *Elevated Innovation: Urban Entrepreneurship and New York City's High Line*. New York: Columbia CaseWorks, Columbia Business School, 2012.

Kimmelman, Michael. "The Climax in a Tale of Green and Gritty: The High Line Opens Its Third and Final Phase." *New York Times*, September 19, 2014.

McGeehan, Patrick. "The High Line Isn't Just a Sight to See; It's Also an Economic Dynamo." *New York Times*, June 5, 2011.

The Tiffany & Co. Foundation, "The Tiffany & Co. Foundation Announces $5 Million Rail Yards Challenge Grant to the High Line." *The Tiffany & Co. Foundation*, June 2011. http://www.tiffanyandcofoundation.org/news/article/High%20Line%202011.aspx.

NOTES

1. 2013 visitorship totaled 4.8 million; 2014 surpassed 6.2 million.

2. Phase 2 of the High Line at the Rail Yards remains under construction at the time of publication, with completion anticipated in 2017. At a future date, the area of the Rail Yards section known as the Western Rail Yards, or the Interim Walkway, will see further repair and restoration, but those plans have not yet been finalized.

3. Transition to the Proposal module was completed in early 2015.

4. This meant that the eastern half of the Rail Yards would receive a full restoration treatment—stripping the High Line down to its bones, repairing any structural deficiencies, laying new concrete foundations, waterproofing, removing lead paint, etc., while the western half would be left largely as David and Hammond had found it in 1999; soil untouched, lead paint encased as opposed to removed, and only a simple walking path, to be known as the Interim Walkway, laid down for visitors and a fence installed to protect the self-seeded landscape.

EIGHT

Building for the Future

Converting Capital Campaign Success into Sustainable Major Gifts

Carl G. Hamm,
Saint Louis Art Museum

Museums undertake capital campaigns to raise funds for new buildings, capital improvements, endowments, or other special projects. Such campaigns are usually considered successful when the campaign's goal is reached or surpassed or once the initiative for which the special gifts have been solicited has been completed. But there can be another important long-term outcome of a successful campaign—a quantum leap in annual giving among a museum's leadership campaign donors.

Conventional wisdom holds that a museum should already have an established base of donors making large annual major gifts before undertaking a campaign. But in real life, museums enter campaigns from all points of organizational maturity, especially in terms of their development programs. Even though a museum has a long, distinguished history or a collection of significant stature, the institution may still have significant unrealized potential for maximizing its capacity for annual giving among its most generous supporters.

This is the story of how one major American art museum successfully translated its capital campaign into a sustainable stream of increased annual giving for the future.

The Saint Louis Art Museum is one of the oldest museums of its type west of the Mississippi River. Founded in 1879, the museum is one of the nation's leading comprehensive art museums with collections that include works of art of exceptional quality representing virtually every culture and time period.

The art museum in St. Louis has experienced three name changes and governance structures over the years, but the underlying constant has been the institution's significant subsidization through a single source of third-party or public funding. Originally created on the campus of

Washington University before moving to its present home, the museum became a department of the City of St. Louis in 1909 and operated as such for more than fifty years. Since 1972, the institution has been a sub-district of the state of Missouri, receiving more than three quarters of its annual operating funding through a unique region-wide property tax. This steady source of taxpayer support fueled the museum's institutional growth and its ability to provide free admission for more than a century. But in the absence of necessity, the institution was not required in its formative years to develop the same type of philanthropic culture or large endowment most art museums require to sustain their daily operations.

Over the course of its history, the museum had received numerous five and six-figure gifts from individuals, but they were mostly one-time, ad hoc contributions to fund acquisitions beyond baseline resources for art purchase. Likewise, when the museum launched what would become its present day general membership program in 1952 and an upper-level giving society recognizing $1,000 annual gifts in 1983, both programs were originally created to fund the purchase of art.[1]

Situation

Around the turn of the twenty-first century, the museum's leadership began to explore an expansion to its century-old landmark building. In 2004, after five years of planning and preparation, the museum launched the leadership phase of a campaign to construct a new building and increase the institution's endowment to support additional costs related to the expanded facility. In the summer of 2011, the museum exceeded its $145 million capital campaign goal, a target that had been increased three times since the first gift to the campaign seven years earlier. By the time the campaign officially closed in 2013, $160 million had been raised through more than 1,500 gifts, including 100 gifts of $100,000 or more from individuals and families.

As one of the steps in creating a financial model for the building project, the museum had developed a multi-year budget projecting the impact of an expanded facility on its operating budget. This exercise, coinciding with other realities facing the museum's public funding model, reinforced how much the museum would need to rely on private support to sustain its operations in the future. The 1972 legislation creating the tax structure supporting the art museum established a ceiling on the percentage that could be levied on taxable property and, by 2011, that cap was close to being reached. This meant that the tax revenue received annually by the museum would soon remain flat—or proportionately decrease over time given inflation—without a significant increase in regional property tax values. A projected increase in annual expenses, a relative decline in the tax funds that had historically sustained the museum, and the identification of a core group of donors who had demonstrated far more capacity and commitment than their previous giving might suggest: these circumstances would form the basis for a new upper-level annual giving program for the museum.

PLANNING

The museum's Beaux Arts Council membership program had been the institution's premier annual giving opportunity for thirty years prior to the campaign. Practically every individual donor of $100,000 or more to the campaign was a longtime member of the group, several since its founding in 1983. Other than special gifts to purchase works of art or establish named endowments, Beaux Arts Council memberships at $5,000 or $10,000 had been considered major annual gifts to the museum.

According to revenue projections in the multi-year operating budget for 2013–2017, unrestricted operating contributions would have to steadily grow, almost doubling within five years following the campaign, to maintain a balanced budget. After reviewing the possible sources of philanthropic funding that might fuel such dramatic growth, it was evident that the greatest opportunity for a quantum leap in the museum's annual giving program would be in the households who had given $100,000 or more through the campaign.

The foundation for the museum's new building had just been poured when the campaign goal was reached in the summer of 2011. Groundbreaking had originally been planned for 2009 with the opening of the expansion set for 2012, which would have coincided neatly with the end of the campaign and provided a natural transition into the museum's next phase. But the unexpected economic downturn of late 2008 had caused the museum to reconsider its plan, and the institution's leadership conservatively chose to delay construction by a year, pushing back an opening until 2013.

Having already met an increased goal three times, it would have been difficult for the museum to justify moving into the community-wide, traditional public phase of a campaign for the next two years. Instead, the museum decided to redirect its efforts into increasing its ongoing base of annual support, using the momentum of the campaign as the catalyst. Multi-year leadership gifts had been committed during the early stages of the campaign and those donors were completing pledge payments in 2010 and 2011. In theory, this group might be ready to step up their annual giving with the proper framework and encouragement.

Table 8.1. Campaign for the Saint Louis Art Museum Giving
by Individuals*

Level	Gifts	Total Raised
$10,000,000+	6	$72,160,000
$2,000,000–$9,999,999	8	$23,884,258
$1,000,000–$1,999,999	10	$11,676,166
$500,000–$999,999	10	$5,387,550
$250,000–$499,999	18	$5,316,582
$100,000–$249,999	48	$5,981,913
Under $100,000	1746	$4,254,110

*As of September 30, 2011

An analysis of the motivation, size, and timing of gifts and pledge payments made by the top 100 campaign donors revealed that most had made
one-time stretch gifts and were only likely to make future major gifts for
special projects, such as the purchase of art. But thirty-four households
emerged as potential candidates to increase their annual membership to
$25,000, $50,000, or $100,000 or more, based on their payment history and
increased engagement.

The Beaux Arts Council program had offered $25,000 and $50,000 levels for years, but the number of members in this realm could be counted
on one hand. Until the campaign, the museum had not been successful
in developing a culture that encouraged giving at these levels, and it
was unlikely that donors would naturally progress into these categories
of annual giving if the program remained status quo. Creating the new
framework for an enhanced upper-level membership program was not
difficult; the challenge would be to establish a case for support and buy-in
from this group who had demonstrated the capacity and interest to give
more but had never considered annual gifts above $5,000 or $10,000.

IMPLEMENTATION

After the $145 million campaign goal had been reached, staff began to in-
troduce the notion of a post-campaign strategy to boost operating support
to the museum's development committee, using the multi-year budget
and campaign gift table as a basis for conversation. PowerPoint presenta-
tions were created with charts and graphs illustrating the rationale of the
museum's need for increased support and the number of donors who had
made significant gifts to the campaign.

A subset of the development committee met several times over the
spring of 2012 to discuss how a new upper-level giving society might be

structured. Should it be a new freestanding group or an extension of the existing Beaux Arts Council? Should there be a new benefits structure? Should the society recognize cumulative annual gifts, including gifts to purchase works of art? Should multi-year commitments be solicited, to engrain a habit of giving at these levels?

The outcome was the recommendation of a new "Leadership Council" program, creating a new $100,000 category and repackaging it with the existing $50,000 and $25,000 levels. Members would receive all the benefits and privileges of Beaux Arts Council membership, with two additions: an annual reception or dinner with the museum director and the exclusive opportunity to travel with the director. Prospects would be asked to make a three-year commitment in exchange for recognition as Founding Members. A structure was now in place, but the case for support needed to be more thoroughly articulated to influence potential donors to make such a dramatic increase in their annual giving. In preparation for formal solicitations, a document was written that framed the challenges of the museum's post-expansion environment in the context of its 133-year history.

In the early fall of 2012, the first Leadership Council prospect was solicited through a meeting with the museum's director, resulting in the first $100,000 multi-year commitment. The prospect also agreed to solicit peers to help establish the new program. Several additional members at the top level followed his lead, but unexpected responses from the subsequent solicited prospects indicated that the broader group might not be ready to embrace the new initiative.

The museum was well known for its financial strength and good stewardship, and this group was particularly aware that the museum's campaign had been the largest for a cultural institution in the city's history. Given the tax support received annually by the museum and the perception of such strong giving through the campaign, based on brief solicitation conversations, donors did not embrace the reality of a need for additional support. Campaign donors had been promised that the museum would not undertake a construction project that would compromise the institution's financial stability. The endowment component of the campaign was supposed to have eliminated this issue, but most endowment gifts received had been deferred commitments without a predictable realization date. This was a difficult point to reinforce with Leadership Council prospects who had made endowment gifts believing they were addressing the museum's increased financial need. The biggest barrier, however, could only be addressed with patience and time. Even though the campaign goal had been met and raised three times, donors were still deeply connected to the museum's construction project emotionally and would need to see the new building completed to feel a sense of closure before being able to consider the museum's need for additional giving.

The museum's rational plan had been to capitalize on the attainment of the campaign goal that had been reached more than a year earlier. In theory, the time to launch a new giving initiative addressing the museum's next phase would be before it had begun. The realization that the museum's donors were not yet focused on the institution's post-construction future was a key revelation that led to the decision to delay active Leadership Council solicitations until after the opening of the expanded campus in June 2013.

RESULTS

When conversations about the Leadership Council resumed after the grand opening, they were met with a much different response than those nine months earlier. Enthusiasm and ownership in the museum were high and the pride donors felt in their philanthropic accomplishment was palpable.

In the fall of 2013, the museum director and chief development officer began to host individual conversations with the original list of Leadership Council prospects. This approach, rather than the peer-driven model of the early solicitations, allowed for more in-depth conversation about the museum's finances and future plans. It also provided a natural forum for the director to invest quality time with the museum's top donors and thank them for their generous past support.

The results were dramatic. Between September 2012 and 2014, the number of members participating in the Leadership Council grew to eighteen members, up from four households at corresponding levels two years earlier. The increase in collective annual giving among these eighteen households grew by more than $500,000, from $255,000 in 2012 to $770,239 two

Table 8.2.   Beaux Arts Council & Leadership
Circle Member Households*

Level	2012	2014
$1,500	219	259
$2,500	96	93
$5,000	54	52
$10,000	21	23
$25,000	3	11
$50,000	1	3
$100,000	0	4

*Figures of September 2012 and September 2014

years later. This represented a quantum leap for an upper-level membership program that had raised, in total, just under $1.1 million in 2012.

LESSONS LEARNED

Apart from the circumstances unique to the Saint Louis Art Museum, there may be several lessons to be gained from this case study.

- First, the strategy a museum undertakes immediately following a campaign can significantly strengthen its annual giving among its top donors in a culture shifting way.
- Those who will be asked to give more or to solicit their peers should be involved in developing the case for support and any changes to the museum's giving programs. This helps establish credibility in the process and forecast potential barriers to future solicitations.
- One-time large gifts to a campaign may demonstrate donors' extraordinary support for the institution and their capacity to make large gifts, but not necessarily indicate their readiness to significantly increase their annual giving without good reason.
- And, as Harold J. Seymour said, "Giving is prompted emotionally and then rationalized. The heart has to prompt the mind to go where logic points the way."[2] A museum's most generous campaign donors may rationally understand a museum's need for increased annual giving, yet may not be ready to emotionally embrace it. Moving too quickly can backfire and can set back critical momentum as a new post-campaign giving program is being launched.

Successful capital campaigns rise to the level of being among a museum's most visible priorities because of the transformational projects they make possible, the large gifts they produce, and the involvement of the institution's top volunteer leadership. But the less glamorous, strategic fundraising that occurs in the post-campaign afterglow can also have a lasting legacy on the ongoing operations of a museum for generations to come. Until the next campaign.

NOTES

1. Over time, the Saint Louis Art Museum has also developed programs to solicit and receive gifts through all the traditional channels of a comprehensive development program, including major and planned gifts; corporate, foundation, and government grants; sponsorships; general membership support and interest

group participation, etc., as well as the solicitation and receipt of individual works of art and private collections through gift and bequest. Because of this article's focus on major gifts from individuals, this abbreviated history was used.

2. Harold J. Seymour, *Designs for Fund-raising: Principles, Patterns [and] Techniques.* New York: McGraw-Hill, 1966, 29.

NINE

Successful Fundraising Strategies for the Academic Museum

Jill Hartz, Jordan Schnitzer
Museum of Art

Fundraising for museums, at the best of times, is hard work. It requires both a short-term plan for annual giving—to keep daily operations in the black and aspirational projects on the horizon—and an end-game strategy for major and planned gifts, often involving years of cultivation, special events, and exclusive benefits for high-net worth prospects and donors. Add to this a parent institution—the university or college—and you have another complex layer of challenges.

Today, it is estimated that there are 2,000 museums, encompassing all manner of collections, at more than 800 academic institutions in the U.S.[1] While their fundraising environment is vastly different from those of free-standing museums, their strategies may have currency for their non-academic brethren. Similar to a diplomat without portfolio, the academic museum is an academic unit without matriculating students and, therefore, alumni, who would comprise the natural pipeline of donors. Unlike athletic departments, museum donors don't have to give annually to get season tickets or prime seats (although we can offer exclusive events now and again).

And that's just for starters. An academic museum may not be in the fortunate position of having its own director of development; indeed, many share fundraising officers whose portfolios include more than the arts—and those officers may not even report to the museum director but to a central vice president or director of development. For most universities, development follows a "team leader" approach, which again privileges academic departments, whose development officers can choose from often thousands of alumni and call themselves the gatekeepers. In contrast, development directors for academic museums often have to wait for the first gifts of art or financial support from alumni before being cleared to approach them.

And what about the board of trustees? Let's replace that independent governing group with an advisory board that looks and acts similarly, but which actually has no legal power or fiduciary responsibility. Usually composed of collectors and major donors, this group is expected to give generously of their advice and resources—without the benefit of hiring the director or setting the museum's goals.

These are only a few of the on-campus issues. Many academic museums also serve as their communities' cultural centers. While area residents become members and visit often, they usually give their larger gifts to those cultural organizations not affiliated with the university: "Doesn't the university take care of its own?" they ask repeatedly.

Those of us who work—and fundraise—for museums in academia have learned how to navigate the often circuitous development protocols we are given and how to make these challenges work for us. We've become master strategists, diplomats, and opportunists. We take what works for non-academic museums and tweak it for our situations, and we make use of the many advantages a university does offer—prospect research, experts in planned giving, and regional officers, among them—to create a tailored plan that engages our on- and off-campus prospects and turns them into annual and major donors.

In this chapter, I share successes based on more than thirty years of experience working in the academic museum field where I have found myself among the smartest, most ingenious development officers any director could hope to hire. My intention is to help my academic colleagues and other museum professionals be more strategic and successful. The examples I provide are case studies from the Jordan Schnitzer Museum of Art (JSMA) at the University of Oregon, where I am now in my seventh year as executive director. I also bring in context from the Association of Academic Museums and Galleries or AAMG (the affiliate academic organization for the Alliance of Academic Museums), for which I serve as president).

GREAT UNIVERSITIES DESERVE GREAT MUSEUMS

This statement—part of a petition—was created by the AAMG in 2008 in response to Brandeis University's decision to sell numerous works in its Rose Art Museum to buoy the coffers of the university, which was reeling from the Madoff scandal. In the end, a group of Brandeis faculty and donors, joined by national museum organizations, were effective in saving the museum and its collections. Those of us in academic museums absorbed at least two lessons from this debacle. First, our museums need to be so closely entwined with as many areas of our campuses as possible—from the president's and provost's offices to academic departments and students—that we can't be excised without the university suffering a traumatic blow. Second, some of our donors are among the university's major donors.

Successful fundraising for the academic museum begins with the recognition that we must treat our university as we would treat our largest donor. In most cases, it is! To be competitive for resources on campus, the museum must have a mission that enhances the university's mission and goals and emphasizes education and access. Likewise, our institutional plans must mirror those of our parents. In an age of fiscal restraint, museums—expensive operations to begin with—must prove their worth.

Academic museums that effectively communicate their educational missions reap the benefits: members of the university's upper administration become critical supporters, advocates, and fundraisers for us. The university's development operation takes its cue from this leadership: officers bring prospects for tours and events, they notice and tell us about art in homes and offices, and they include us in strategy sessions. The momentum builds.

At the JSMA, I report to two entities within the university—the vice president of advancement and the provost and senior vice president. An organizational model that's been in effect now for six years, this dual reporting structure, while controversial in some museum circles, gives me the best of both worlds: an academic supervisor at the highest level, who can help further our educational outreach and student engagement and the senior fundraising officer of the university for whom the museum is part of his core operation.

CREATING YOUR ALUMNI

One of the seemingly insurmountable issues for academic museums is our lack of alumni. That doesn't mean that alumni aren't involved with us—as members, donors of art, advisory board members, and docents—because they are. But most of the time, they have to self-identify their museum interest. While occasionally we benefit from development officers, friends, and other alumni who tell us about a potential supporter, more often we conduct research the old-fashioned way—delving through season programs and annual reports from cultural organizations in communities rife with alumni, reviewing filed contact reports, and getting to know our members and asking them to give more. In this way, we methodically build our alumni pipeline.

But what if we had *our own* alumni? For many years, the JSMA offered a free membership program to students on campus. All we asked them to provide was their email addresses, which we used to invite them to preview openings and other special events. As student members, they also received discounts at our store and café. Our student membership grew over time (from 200 seven years ago to more than 2,000 now) but not as quickly as we hoped.

Last year, we successfully applied for a GTF (graduate teaching fellow) for administrative support. Sarah Turner, in her final year as an MA student in arts and administration, became our first GTF and student membership president. Working with a cadre of undergraduate and graduate students from departments across the university, she conducted a student survey, created bylaws, chaired regularly meetings, and developed a series of three programs *by* students and *for* students: a performance art evening, a juried art exhibition responding to a major exhibition on view, and an acapella music event. The Jordan Schnitzer Museum of Art Student Membership Advisory Council (JSMAC) hosted membership tables at our openings and university events, and has thus far attracted more than 2,000 student members in 2014. Its application for status as an official student organization came before the Student Council this year, and was approved, thereby opening a new funding opportunity. Our second GTF starts this fall. Until JSMAC is self-sustaining, a student position focused on building student membership is essential for continued success. This year, we'll also develop a plan for our graduating class, including alumni memberships and reunions.

Student engagement isn't driven only by JSMAC. Each year, about sixty students work in the museum as receptionists, gallery monitors, event staff, and departmental support. They serve as paid employees, volunteers, or interns earning academic credit. We hope that some will work at the museum throughout their time on campus. Therefore, we try to hire students early in their matriculation so we can build that bond with them over time.

We also attract students through their professors. Recently, we invited faculty to teach their courses in the museum, and we started an academic support grant program (we asked schools to match our support, which is then matched by the provost) given competitively to faculty who use the museum as a site of learning. During 2012–2013, Danielle Knapp, our McCosh Associate Curator, and Professor Phaedra Livingstone (AAD/ Museum Certificate) designed a year-long series of three courses that resulted in an exhibition and publication on Pierre Daura, an artist well represented in our collection. This year, Professor Akiko Walley, a Japanese art historian, and Anne Rose Kitagawa, our chief curator and curator of Asian art, will team up on a similar sequence, resulting in a major exhibition and publication of the Wadsworth Collection of Japanese prints, a recent gift to the museum. Particularly for young scholars interested in pursuing museum careers, we find that these classes can be life-changing experiences because they offer students a deep understanding of and appreciation for museum practice.

WHEN ALUMNI MAKE THE CASE

Now that we have cultivated our administration, which increasingly supports and promotes our academic innovations and partnerships across the curriculum, and we have a strategy in place for faculty and student engagement, we need to address alumni giving. We work hard to make the museum a familiar and favorite place by hosting board meetings for our university's foundation, the alumni center, and university trustees. We give special tours to their spouses. We offer free admission during home games. Because my curators and I travel internationally in support of our far-ranging collections and exhibitions, we speak to alumni groups—about the university and the museum. And alumni tell alumni, particularly when you have such a close-knit body of university supporters as the Ducks!

We have found that our advisory board, which is called a Leadership Council, is one of the most effective ways to engage major alumni collectors and donors. Once ground rules are clear—advisory means *advisory*—we create meaningful opportunities for them to participate in the life and planning of the museum that makes them essential to our success. They form "Action Teams" for major exhibitions and other projects with the purpose of identifying and engaging targeted constituents, developing programs and evaluation, and raising funds to realize them. They serve on acquisitions, long-range planning, program support, and development committees. And while we might not be able to lure the major university donor onto our board, we might do just as well with his or her spouse.

CAPITAL CAMPAIGN SUCCESS

Because our museum is more than eighty years old, it has become a university institution. From alumni, I regularly hear what the museum meant to them during their student days: a respite from the pressures of academia, a place to go to impress your date, or a location to be inspired by and learn from art.

The power of nostalgia can be a powerful kick-starter for a capital campaign. In the fall of 2014, on the eve of the university's campaign announcement, one of the major donors to the university and a long-time member of the Leadership Council announced that she and her husband were making a pledge to build the museum's new visitor center. While they have given generously to many areas of the university, the museum has always held a special place in her heart since her student days. She tells the story of how she and her friends would sneak into the museum on campus at a time when our facility was less than hospitable; nonetheless, as students, she and her friends would enjoy our galleries and courtyard until a museum employee would notice their presence. Then, they'd sprint away.

Our museum has, of course, changed enormously since that time. Today, we welcome and teach thousands of students annually and provide an exciting, enriching, and welcoming experience for every visitor. Still, we are hampered by the architecture and disconnect between our austere first floor entrance and the magnificent galleries and art that lie in wait on our second floor. Thanks to donors, we are now planning for a spectacular new pavilion that will entice students across campus and visitors from near and far.

ENGAGING COMMUNITY: LIVING LEGACIES

During my first six years, I had focused intently on connecting the museum to the university's academic mission, creating a strategic plan and building an effective advisory board. In 2013, it was time to build our off-campus engagement. My curators and I conceived of one of its most complicated and ambitious exhibitions to date—*Living Legacies: The JSMA at 80*—a follow-up to our seventy-fifth anniversary show, *Lasting Legacies*, which honored the gifts and individuals that had made the museum what it had become. For *Living Legacies*, we wanted to look to our future and uncover both art treasures and potential new supporters. The exhibition was expansive, taking over the museum with 300 pieces from eighty collectors. It became one of the highest attended shows ever as lenders brought in their friends and families and community members came to see what surprises lived among them. Collectors gave tours and enjoyed a series of connoisseurship panels—and they continue to be involved, giving both art and financial support.

Our off-campus outreach, which generates grants and foundation support, goes far beyond collectors. Our arts education programs in Oregon schools, family activities, special programs for challenged populations, and film and music events—all affirm that we are a good neighbor and worthy of support. Interested in reaching specific audiences, we aim to work more closely with minority populations. To this end, we have developed a Latino Engagement Plan that looks at building new and diverse audiences and hopes to assure the museum's sustainability as demographics continue to change.

A FEW KEY RECOMMENDATIONS

This chapter does not attempt to be comprehensive in laying out an effective fundraising plan for academic museums. What works for me may not work for you, and vice versa. In general, however, the following recommendations will be useful to all of us who are dedicated to making our museums strong today and tomorrow.

1. If you get substantial funding from your university or college, treat it like the most important donor you have. It is. Spread that cultivation broadly, from the president on down.
2. Exemplify the teaching museum model. The more you enhance the university's curriculum across campus, the more support you will receive on campus. Have students make your case for you. When students share their learning, everyone listens and understands what a teaching museum is.
3. Find creative ways to create and cultivate your own alumni.
4. Be patient. Don't expect major gifts to happen quickly. When people give you their art, they're giving you something precious.
5. Create an advisory board of alumni and community friends who are or will be your major supporters.
6. Train your staff. Like marketing, fundraising is something almost everyone in the museum needs to do. Find out whom your staff knows and would like to cultivate.
7. Advocate for a development officer independent of the college or university, if you don't already have one. Unless you don't need to raise money, you need someone working full-time on your behalf. That person needs to supervise membership/annual giving and events staff, work closely with other development officers at the university, plan prospect visits with the director.
8. Always diversify your funding as one area may go away and others will have to fill in. Seek individual support and major gifts, write grants, and prepare foundation proposals. Even small grants, especially when they're from your state arts council, can give credibility and leverage other resources.
9. Hold events where parking is easy to find. If this isn't possible, reserve parking for your guests.
10. Participate in your community. Take part in Chamber of Commerce, civic, and arts events. Universities can seem remote and insular, so make sure your community sees you as an integral partner in its life and vitality.

RESOURCE RECOMMENDATIONS

Websites and Blogs

Association of Fundraising Professionals. http://www.afpnet.org
Future Fundraising Now. http://www.futurefundraisingnow.com/
Guidestar. "Fundraising's Four Magic Questions: Answer These and the Gift if Yours." http://www2.guidestar.org/rxa/news/articles/2007/fundraisings-four-magic-questions-answer-these-and-the-gift-is-yours.aspx?articleId=1108Harrison, Jon. "Nonprofit Fundraising Web Resources" http://staff.lib.msu.edu/harris23/grants/4fcelec.htm
Network for Good. http://www.fundraising123.org
Non Profit Resource Center. http://www.nprcenter.org/
Perry, Gail. "Fired Up Fundraising." http://www.gailperry.com/resource-center/blog/
Philanthropy Journal. http://www.philanthropyjournal.org/

Books

Brophy, Sarah S. *Is Your Museum Grant-Ready?* Lanham, MD: AltaMira Press, 2005.
Hopkins, Karen Brooks, and Carolyn Stolper Friedman. *Successful Fundraising for Arts and Cultural Organizations*. Phoenix: The Oryx Press, 1997.
Howlett, Susan. *Boards on Fire! Inspiring Leaders to Raise Money Joyfully*. Seattle: Word and Raby, 2010.
Johnson, Kevin. *The Power of Legacy and Planned Gifts*. San Francisco: John Wiley & Sons, 2010.
Rich, Patricia, and Dana Hines. *Membership Development*. Sudbury, MA: Jones and Bartlett Publishers, 2006.

NOTE

1. Danilov, Victor J. *America's College Museums: Handbook & Directory*. Second Edition. Amenia, NY: Grey House Publishing, 2011: Preface.

TEN

Relevance and Twenty-First Century Fundraising Fundamentals

James G. Leventhal,[1] the Contemporary
Jewish Museum, and Irina Zeylikovich,
Bay Area Discovery Museum

This chapter seeks to address the issue of engaging the next generation of philanthropists in supporting museums throughout times of crisis, uncertainty, and shifting donor perceptions. Our contention is that fundraisers can leverage and respond to ever-present conditions such as crisis, uncertainty, and shifting donor perceptions—often now referred to as "the new normal"—through the age-old nonprofit essentials of relevance, relationships, and resources. As professionals working in fundraising, we offer case studies from our own institutions: the Contemporary Jewish Museum (The CJM) and Bay Area Discovery Museum, with a focus on event-based engagement and the goal of connecting donors to programs across the museum landscape.

Colleagues write persuasively about fundraising and the twenty-first century challenges and commensurate opportunities. For instance, Kim Klein in *Fundraising in Times of Crisis,* identifies threats to organizational existence, primarily from the post–September 11 economic crises, the size of the nonprofit sector, and the "erosion of public trust in the sector brought on by scandals and perceptions of mismanagement."[2] Noted museum researcher John Falk also observes that "although museums should be among the resource rich leaders in this expanding era of learning, they are in danger of residing on the sidelines or quietly disappearing—unless they can reexamine old assumptions and make dramatic changes in practice."[3]

The very real effects of the post-2008 economic crisis are evident in the Bay Area, particularly for arts organizations. The nature of the crisis is made manifest by the fact that several important arts organizations have closed within the last several years, including: the Museum of Craft and Folk Art in 2012[4]; New Langton Arts in 2010; and Intersection for the Arts, which shuttered its arts practice in 2014. Perhaps these closings are a natural resizing of the number of actual offerings on the market; but, still, it

_.....nt to explore how, as fundraisers, we can have an impact as the industry responds to perceived and real paradigm shifts in cultural funding in America in the twenty-first century. While many organizations would instinctively trim expenses in response to such circumstances, Klein instead advises that we "use this crisis as a way to create new income streams. Cutting expenses will not provide any permanent solution to your crisis, nor will it move you in a new direction as an organization."[5] Put simply, as fundraisers, we can work hard to make a difference.

RELEVANCE

In response to a recent *Huffington Post* article titled, "The New WhatsApp Billionaires and the Future of Philanthropy,"[6] the Center for the Future of Museums wrote that the next generation of donors has "increased expectations for outcomes-based measurement of the effects of their giving . . . more focus on spending down a foundation's [sic] wealth in return for quick, tangible results . . . [and] a desire to influence policy through political giving."[7] Coupled with the recent economic downturn, these increased expectations can seem daunting; yet as museum fundraisers, it is our charge to translate this form of desired engagement into action and to motivate these donors to be a part of our cause. We must ensure that the work of our museums is presented in a meaningful way, and that the work we are doing is significant. These shifts are significant as moves toward science, technology, engineering, and math (STEM) funding become priorities in government programs and across higher education institutions; and compelling statements about social responsibility by lead philanthropists such as Bill Gates are directed against cultural investment. Gates was recently quoted as having questioned why people would "donate money to build a new wing for a museum rather than spend it on preventing illnesses that can lead to blindness."[8] As Falk notes, "Our mandate for today must be to build the capacity of our institutions to change with the times and reestablish our critical purpose in society. . . . As we ask, 'Why do museums exist?' . . . we need to see ourselves as institutions embedded in a world that is rapidly changing before our eyes."[9]

Significant ways to keep donors involved have always been the defining challenge and the ultimate opportunity in advancing the cause of museums. Here we examine participation through event-based engagement and demonstrated impact. Time becomes an increasingly precious commodity and, as noted above, many donors truly see themselves more as "investors" than "donors"—all the more so for millennials. According to Amy Webb of Webbmedia Group, "It's just semantics: donation vs. investment. But I think to a millennial, who's grown up in a very different world, one that's more participatory because of the digital tools that we have, to them they want to feel like they're making an investment. Not just that they're investing their capital, but they're investing emotionally."[10]

Relevance should be focused but not needy, and should come from a place of plenty. Despite an overall retrenchment we have, in fact, seen growth in giving in the cultural sector. As noted in the American Alliance of Museum's Center for the Future of Museum's (CFM) research:

> TrendsWatch 2013[11] [examined] the "Changing Face of Giving." Though the economy, and giving overall, continues to rebound, there's wide agreement that we aren't going to return to the world that existed pre-2008. We are seeing a fundamental shift in who has money to give, the criteria used to select who to give to, and what causes actually get support.[12]

Further, CFM reports that "the good news is that giving to Cultural, Arts and Humanities (which included museums), increased over 7 percent last year. That is twice the average increase for giving overall. So not only are museums rebounding, we are rebounding faster than others in the non-profit sector."[13] Demonstrating how one gift has helped leverage another, for example, can increase donor confidence that their investment is supporting a strong, stable organization.

The rebound is particularly evident for children's museums, which can leverage the increasing media and federal focus on early childhood education of the last several years. The Bay Area Discovery Museum has used this opportunity to utterly transform its fundraising events. Playdate, the museum's annual gala, was transformed in 2013 when Bay Area Discovery Museum leadership and development staff undertook a drastic revisioning of the Playdate experience and changed the event's location from a hotel in downtown San Francisco back to the museum's site in Sausalito. With engaging themes, passed hors d'oeuvres, cocktails, and music and entertainment acts such as Velocity Circus, donors are treated to a Bay Area Discovery Museum transformed beneath an illuminated Golden Gate Bridge. Playdate became a fun complement to the family and community focused fundraising events held throughout the year, recognizing that a diversity of experiences in event fundraising keeps donors engaged.

Drastic changes of core elements to your institution's single largest source of revenue can be intimidating and fraught with risk, yet if they are informed by donor desires and supported by leadership and the museum's board, they can certainly be successful. In the case of the Bay Area Discovery Museum, the change in venue heralded a significant diversification to the suite of fundraising events, and a subsequent decrease of risk as a result of a broader revenue stream. The museum's fundraising stream now includes the following three events, in addition to Playdate:

- Creativity Forum: a thought leadership luncheon held in San Francisco each spring.
- Goblin Jamboree: a weekend-long Halloween family fundraiser held at the museum each October, with price points geared toward museum members and the wider community. Goblin Jamboree also features a Sponsor Breakfast to engage museum donors, which includes exclusive activities and early entry to the festival.
- Snowdays: new in 2014, a three-day family fundraiser at the museum in December featured real snow in Sausalito and themed programming around the science of snow.

Other transformations include a shift in the format for Creativity Forum. Originally a seated lunch during a single keynote speaker's address, in 2015 Creativity Forum will become a moderated conversation between two experts on themes relevant to the Bay Area Discovery Museum's mission. Snow Days, an entirely new program, launched in December 2014, provided another opportunity for intergenerational programming, a facet proving increasingly popular among the museum's supporters.

Success is measured through a number of metrics, which allows for analysis beyond the bottom line of funds contributed. Beginning in 2013, the Bay Area Discovery Museum started tracking key performance indicators (KPIs), tailored to be relevant for each department. Development KPIs provide a richer picture of team efforts beyond goal metrics, and include numbers of participants, new relationships formed, new sponsors acquired, conversions to higher levels of giving, and engagement with event activities. These measures are reported to the board as part of event planning to ensure board engagement, and through summaries during post-event debriefs.

Relevance is really the most important operative term. If your leadership is excited and informed then they will bring their friends and associates to the table (relationships) and model the giving behavior (resources) that makes the work you do together possible. It is an important way to remind your donors of the relevance of your organization—events are often when they can attend, and so it is important that your museum's relevance is literally on display during these occasions.

At the Contemporary Jewish Museum, the launch event for the exhibition *Do Not Destroy: Trees, Art and Jewish Thought an Exhibition and The Dorothy Saxe Invitational* (2012) was ticketed as a benefit, finding that real "value" increases both actual and perceived value. By offering a ticket, something tangible and the opportunity to invest at every level, guests are more likely to take pride in participation—to attend and promote the event among their peers. The exhibition *Do Not Destroy* included an important artist's invitational component. For this, the CJM reached out to those artists with free tickets for the opening event. The turnout was terrific with hundreds of guests. The food was themed in its presentation, tastefully conceived by the CJM's events manager, Taylor Spitzer. Success was borne out in sheer numbers, mission fulfillment reaching new audiences and in signature, local press. *San Francisco Chronicle* society columnist Leah Garchik attended the opening and wrote, "Often at openings in established institutions, the crowd's dominated by Boomers turning into coots (count me in), causing concern among supporters: what'll happen in a few years? At the CJM, the tree-loving art gobblers included folks with canes and folks with tattoos, as well as artists . . . admiring each other's work."[14] It was a terrific point of pride that the intentional work we were doing at the CJM was being recognized and highlighted—bringing multiple generations together as active participants in a mission-driven activity that also happened to be well funded.

RELEVANCE AND COMMUNICATION

Further, in terms of relevance and beyond events, it is important that all audiences from the board to the broader public are aware of your institution's impact. Boards must be helpful here, and must feel equally qualified and equipped to serve as advocate, ambassador, and asker. To give your board the tools and information—in fact, the confidence—that they need to properly represent your organization, it is important to have standard reporting on metrics. As in any investment made in the for-profit or nonprofit worlds, lead investors need an understanding for the overall success and pace of growth of an organization, or in the case of a nonprofit how best to measure the value of the investment against the stated mission of the organization. Financial transparency is critical, along with clear and concise reporting around participation and impact, including number of visitors and patrons served. Certain intangibles, like impressions in the media and online participation can have the greatest impact; and it is so important to provide additional qualitative feedback to enhance the board's overall understanding. This kind of information should also be shared broadly among the entire organization, and continually with the public beyond the 990 financials. Terrific examples of this include the use of online dashboards at museums such as Washington State Historical Society and the Indianapolis Museum of Art.

RELEVANCE, FUNDRAISING, AND PROGRAMMING

Another important way to communicate with the new generation of philanthropic leaders is to be sure that they are connected to program staff. Many of these donors have built their own companies. They have developed horizontally focused organizational structures. They want to know what frontline staff think, how each customer is being treated, and what program-matic leaders have in terms of content-based assets. This kind of dialogue and partnership between development and program staff is not necessarily built into museum structures, yet fundraiser Rory Green notes that it is in-herently possible to establish:

> Make fundraising fun for your program staff. Give them credit for the work they are doing. Recognize them often, publicly, privately. Be sincere—and don't be shy with your thanks. Be specific about the difference their help has made. Show them how they have helped get the donation, and how that donation will help the cause. When they host a donor for a tour, when a prospect they identified makes a gift, celebrate them. Do you have little ritu-als to celebrate big gifts? Include the program staff. Let them ring the bell.[15]

As evidenced above in the program and content driven activities, both at the Bay Area Discovery Museum and the Contemporary Jewish Museum, engagement of program staff is essential. There is a significant bond cre-ated in the development of these activities, providing exposure to the mission throughout the fundraising work—from inception to execution, with program staff as partners all along the way.

CONCLUSION

Rob Stein, deputy director of the Dallas Museum of Art, recently wrote about the new generation of philanthropists' desires for outcomes and deliverables. In a recent piece posted on Medium entitled "Museums . . . So What?"[16] he posits:

> The effective altruism movement is not in and of itself a bad thing. In fact, a community of serious investors who are committed to seeing true and de-monstrable impact from their giving can hardly be faulted. The problem lies with the cultural sector's inability to mount a compelling case of evidence to convince these *"effective altruists"* that tangible and meaningful benefit does in-deed result from investing in the arts and culture. Our impassioned arguments about how museums can change lives and bring communities closer together are all well-and-good, but they mean very little to a data-driven philanthropist if we cannot bring supporting evidence with us to prove our point.[17]

As museum development professionals, we must focus on the inherent value of our institutions' work—it is the differentiating element, the value proposition, and the most compelling case. We are best when we tap that nerve, then pull at the heartstrings through honest discovery and asser-tion of shared values.

RESOURCES

Websites

Center for the Future of Museums http://www.aam-us.org/resources/center-for-the-future-of-museums
Robert J. Stein on Medium: https://medium.com/@rjstein
Michael Peter Edson on Medium: https://medium.com/@mpedson
Western Museums Association blog: http://westmuse.org/blog

Books

Anderson, Gail. *Reinventing the Museum: Historical and Contemporary Perspectives on the Paradigm Shift*. Lanham, MD: Rowman & Littlefield, 2006.
Falk, John H., and Beverly K. Sheppard, *Thriving in the Knowledge Age: New Business Models for Museums and Other Cultural Institutions*. Lanham, MD: Rowman & Littlefield, 2006.
Grace, Kay Sprinkel. *Beyond Fundraising: New Strategies for Nonprofit Innovation and Investment*. San Francisco: John Wiley & Sons, 2005.
Hopkins, Karen Brooks, and Carolyn Stolper Friedman. *Successful Fundraising for Arts and Cultural Organizations*. Westport, CT: Greenwood Publishing Group, 1997.
Kanter, Beth, and Katie Delahaye Paine. *Measuring the Networked Nonprofit*. San Francisco: Jossey-Bass, 2012.
Klein, K. *Fundraising in Times of Crisis*. San Francisco: Jossey-Bass, 2004.
Tempel, Eugene R., ed. *Hank Rosso's Achieving Excellence in Fundraising*. San Francisco: John Wiley & Sons, 2010.

NOTES

1. In November 2014, James G. Leventhal assumed the position of Director of Development at the Exploratorium in San Francisco.

2. Kim Klein, *Fundraising in Times of Crisis*. San Francisco: Jossey-Bass, 2004, 2.

3. John H. Falk and Beverly K. Sheppard, *Thriving in the Knowledge Age: New Business Models for Museums and Other Cultural Institutions*. Lanham, MD: Rowman & Littlefield, 2006, ix.

4. "SF Museum of Craft and Folk Art Closing," September 20, 2012, accessed October 19, 2014, http://www.sfgate.com/art/article/SF-Museum-of-Craft-and-Folk-Art-closing-3882473.php.

5. Falk and Sheppard, 41.

6. David Callahan, "The New WhatsApp Billionaires and the Future of Philanthropy," *Huffington Post*, February 22, 2014, accessed October 25, 2014, http://www.huffingtonpost.com/david-callahan/whatsapp-billionaires_b_4840361.html.

7. Elizabeth Merritt, "Update on Philanthropy," American Alliance of Museum's *Center for the Future of Museums* blog, accessed October 19, 2014, http://futureofmuseums.blogspot.com/2014/08/update-on-philanthropy.html.

8. Richard Waters, "An Exclusive Interview with Bill Gates," *The Financial Times*, November 1, 2013, accessed November 17, 2014, http://on.ft.com/18Jatka

9. Falk and Sheppard, 49–50.

10. Elise Hu, "How Millennials Are Reshaping Charity and Online Giving," West Virginia Public Broadcasting, October 14, 2014, accessed October 19, 2014 http://wvpublic.org/post/how-millennials-are-reshaping-charity-and-online-giving.

11. American Alliance of Museums, *TrendsWatch*, accessed October 19, 2014, http://www.aam-us.org/resources/center-for-the-future-of-museums/projects-and-reports/trendswatch.

12. Merritt, "Update on Philanthropy."

13. Ibid.

14. Leah Garchik, "Dancing to the Rhythms of Politics," *San Francisco Chronicle*, February 20, 2012, accessed October 16, 2014, http://www.sfgate.com/entertainment/garchik/article/Dancing-to-the-rhythms-of-politics-3343006.php.

15. See http://www.pamelagrow.com/4267/5-steps-unlocking-hidden-fundraisers-a-practical-guide-working-better-with-program-staff-raising-more-money/, accessed October 18, 2014. Here, guest author Rory Green is described as follows: "Guest blogger, Rory Green has been fundraising since the age of 10, when she volunteered to help run her school's annual Bike-A-Thon for juvenile cancer research. Fundraising became her vocation at 14, when she lost a friend to Leukemia. Rory is Senior Development Officer at Canada's BCIT Foundation by day, and infamous as the brilliant *Fundraiser Grrl* by night." See http://fundraisergrrl.tumblr.com/.

16. Robert J. Stein, "Museums . . . So What?" CODE | WORDS: Technology and Theory in the Museum, accessed October 19, 2014 https://medium.com/code-words-technology-and-theory-in-the-museum/museums-so-what-7b4594e72283.

17. Stein goes on to make tangible recommendations in his post, such as, Consider what could happen for a moment if Museums were able to document—like universities do—our creative alumni? With the technology currently at our disposal, why are we only so focused on patron management systems (CRM by another name) that track the money people donate to us? What if we focused instead on keeping a catalog and evidence of the creative imprint our audiences are exposed to and the impact they make on the world. Such a catalogue could effectively illustrate the museum's imprint on the formation of creative ideas and creative professionals and their resulting innovation across a multitude of fields. This alumni creativity database could be a proof-text for the role of museums in the formation of creativity and a boon for fundraising linked to this important outcome.

ELEVEN

Institutionalizing Innovation at the Toledo Museum of Art

Amy Gilman,
Toledo Museum of Art

The Toledo Museum of Art (TMA) was founded April 18, 1901, by seven incorporators that included an attorney, an architect, an industrialist, a realtor, a journalist, and two artists. Each of them focused on their shared vision of creating an institution that would enhance the community with art and art education. More than a century later, the Toledo Museum of Art is considered one of the finest museums in the country, both for the quality and for the comprehensiveness of its collections. Thanks to the benevolence of its founders, as well as the continued support of its members, the Toledo Museum of Art remains a privately endowed, nonprofit institution and opens its collections to the public—free of charge—310 days a year.

BACKGROUND (FALL 2010)

In September 2010, Dr. Brian Kennedy was hired as director and was charged by the board with putting together a draft strategic plan for the museum. While financially stable, TMA had been hit hard by the recession, the recent departure of its previous director, and a year of interim leadership. It was by no means in crisis, but the institution, like many in a period of leadership transition, was rudderless.

Kennedy immediately began a comprehensive strategic planning process that included large open-question sessions with key stakeholder groups including: staff, board, volunteers, docents, women's auxiliary groups, security, and faculty of the University of Toledo. Over the course of six weeks some 400 people participated in brainstorming sessions at which the museum leadership gathered responses to ten questions.[1] All 3,400 responses were synthesized and used to formulate five strategic objectives that became the foundation of the museum's new strategic plan. These objectives—expanding access to the collection, teaching visual literacy, increasing visibility, developing museum assets, and working with artists—were incorporated into a four-year strategic plan implemented in July 2011. In addition to the five strategic objectives, the tenets listed below have served as practical guiding principles in the subsequent implementation of the strategic plan.

FOUNDATIONAL TO THE TMA APPROACH

1. First, know what is the central core of your institution; do not try to make your institution something it is not.
2. People are your best assets.
3. Money follows good ideas.
4. *Strategy* (what you are going to do), *Structure* (how museum resources are configured in order to achieve strategy), *Staffing* (do you have the right people, in the right positions in order to implement strategy?) . . . repeat, repeat, repeat.
5. *Plan, Implement, Evaluate* . . . repeat, repeat, repeat.
6. Once you have your strategic plan focus your *activities* only on your objectives. Ruthlessly stop doing activities that are not relevant to the objectives or take you away from your institutional core (i.e., don't try to be everything to everyone).

Fundamental to the strategic plan was the necessity of truly examining how to structure a museum in the twenty-first century—honoring history and tradition, while embracing new technology and leveraging new thinking around innovative management and fundraising practices. In particular, there was recognition of the need to expand our funding base. All museums seek to be permanent. In order to achieve permanence, they must be sustainable.[2] Current models for funding are no longer adequate to ensure such sustainability and permanence. Ensuring sustainability is only achieved through relevance to your current and future constituents and donors. Relevance requires innovative thinking about *how* we do what we do, how we *fund* what we do, as well as appealing not only to the current generation of donors but our future funding base as well. Traditional models of sponsorship and fundraising are not necessarily appealing to a new generation of donors and visitors. A harsh reality is that if art museums continue to rely solely on the fundraising strategies that have been successful over the past forty years, they will face an increasingly, even perilously, smaller donor base as they become less and less relevant to a new generation of donors. Museums must adapt. This is not a new message. Many museums are experimenting with different ways of tackling these issues. The TMA approach looked not just at new programming, but rather focused attention on how best to structure the staff in order to achieve needed relevance through realization of the strategic objectives.

THE STRATEGY IS SET (FALL 2011)

Now for the structure. When Kennedy arrived at the TMA, there was a traditional museum departmental organizational structure in place. The first change made to the organization was to switch to a matrix structure that maintained traditional departments but pushed the strategic objectives across the whole organization. This initial change resulted in several others: members of the Executive Team (director, COO, associate director, chief curator, director of marketing and communications, director of development) were assigned to direct one of the five objectives. Then the museum reconfigured the budget to allocate dollars to the objectives rather than to departments. (Authority and importance had to be invested in meeting the objectives, not on maintaining functioning of the traditional departmental activities.) In addition, the implementation, management, and communication efforts of the Executive Team were bolstered by the creation of a Senior Management Team (consisting of the director, associate director, and COO) who addressed strategy and planning. An entire staff restructure in January 2013 then ushered in an entirely new way of looking at the organization (Fig. 11.1). The "butterfly chart," divides the organization into two parts ("Content" overseen by the associate director and "Resources" overseen by the COO). There were a number of important guidelines we used when developing the plan for restructuring the staff:

- How should this museum be structured *now* in order to best achieve its mission?
- What is important for the museum to be doing right now? And do we have someone whose job is to do that?
- Do not accept "we've always done it this way" as a reason to keep things the same.
- Always *ask* the most uncomfortable question and *engage* a discussion around it. If the question makes you uncomfortable, it is the right question to ask. Being open to difficult questions allows you to see places where resources are not being utilized fully, and allows you to be open to new ideas and ways of challenging long held beliefs about "how we do things around here."

TOLEDO MUSEUM OF ART

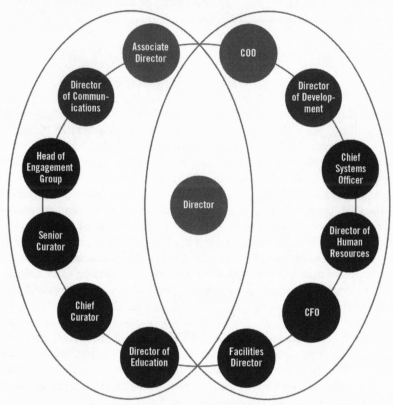

Figure 11.1. This "butterfly" organizational chart was the foundation of the institutional restructuring that took place at the TMA in early 2013.
Courtesy of the Toledo Museum of Art.

Examining each aspect of the institution with these things in mind may very well result in affirmation: "yes, keep things the way they are." But it also, and equally importantly, may result in a renewed sense of how best to leverage an important asset, or best utilize a department, or help see something familiar in an entirely new way. If you commit to really examining your structure you must remind yourself, and everyone around you, that nothing, and no one is sacred. This is about being clear-sighted on what is best for the institution, not what is comfortable or expedient. You may decide to slow down or speed up the pace of change in implementation, but should never sacrifice the long-term view.

IMPLEMENTATION

At many museums "staff restructuring" is synonymous with "saving money" or "cutting staff." It is important to note here that while budget issues may be a driver in decision-making, the moment in which you have a budget crisis, or in which there is an economic downturn, is probably not the point at which you are able to think objectively about what the institution needs as far as a healthy and sustainable number of staff and where they might be situated. In that instance, a restructure is driven by a crisis or by the anticipation of a crisis.

In the case of the TMA, the goal of the restructure was not to cut numbers or dollars and while it did result in eleven initial staff departures, the total FTE (full time equivalent) staff number did not change. Positions and their placement within the organization did change and, as a result, we had to make difficult decisions about people who were longtime employees but whose skills no longer matched with the museum's current needs. When the large-scale staff restructure was undertaken in January 2013 we were prepared for critique, and for adjustment based on feedback. In fact, the first adjustment to the plan occurred mere weeks after rolling it out.

The senior leadership made an important decision around this particular restructuring plan: we kept the planning group very small. Only three people (director, associate director, and COO) participated, which allowed for fairly fast and dramatic change but did not result in as much buy-in over the whole staff during implementation of the restructuring. That was the tradeoff. We could have garnered greater staff buy-in (as we did with the initial strategic plan discussions when Kennedy first arrived at the museum), but the pace of change would have been much slower, and the level of change not as substantial.

In the implementation of a staff restructuring there are some key points to keep in mind:

1. Accept the pros/cons of the choices you made on the planning side to balance speed, pace, and scope of change. No one will embrace every decision made positively.
2. Take the long view when rolling new initiatives out. Make adjustments when it becomes clear they are needed, but do not lose sight of the end goal.
3. There will be staff departures. See these departures as opportunities, not as crises. When several department head positions became vacant, the TMA solicited outside evaluations of the departments. Senior management, and the eventual new hire, were given a report that could serve as a departmental road map for changes needed to ensure best practice and make sure the department was contributing to fulfilling the museum's strategic objectives.

Highlights of some of the changes implemented at TMA with restructuring

On each side of the new "butterfly" organizational chart were several familiar departments, as well as a new department that combined several elements of the traditional museum structure. These were the Systems Group and the Visitor Engagement Group. Specifically, in the case of the Systems Group, we expanded beyond the Information Technology (IT) and related functions personnel to include the Registrar's office, the Library, and the Archives into the area. This incorporation was in recognition that those three areas are, in essence, information management groups; and as such, the museum needed them to embrace systems thinking and digital tools in order to better integrate all our collections management systems together and update our procedures. Our determination was that the best way to facilitate the embrace of that kind of change would be to have the areas report through a Systems Group rather than keeping them within the Curatorial Department.

Other changes of note included the implementation of a weekly report system whereby each member of the Executive Team (ET) drafts a status report on Friday about their department and any other issues they feel need to be addressed by senior management. These reports have proved invaluable not only in providing insight into what each department is working through in a given week, but also all together they allow for a weekly "snapshot" of the whole institution. The reports then serve as the basis of the agenda for the senior management meeting on Mondays, and subsequently inform the conversation at the ET meeting on Wednesdays.

These regular Monday and Wednesday meetings are now enhanced by the implementation of a rotating executive-in-charge for each weekend. Each member of the ET takes responsibility for weekend duty. The executive-in-charge calendar is posted publicly for the staff. Each executive-in-charge is required to be present at the museum the equivalent of a full working day and must spend a significant amount of that time "on the floor." That individual then conducts a "weekly briefing" on Tuesday afternoon with frontline staff to bring forward any feedback from the previous week. The executive-in-charge reports on the weekend and the briefing at the Wednesday ET meeting. This process has raised the profile of the executive level management with the rest of the staff, and each ET member has also reported an increased familiarity and understanding of the daily workings of the museum and the issues our front-of- house staff face during the museum's open hours. In sum, these activities allow for more effective flow of communication and provide a conduit for issues to come up and be dealt with quickly and proactively.

ASSESSMENT, NEXT STEPS, AND LESSONS LEARNED

Overall, the museum is in a very different place than it was in 2010—and therefore this next strategic planning process must, by necessity, fit with where the institution is now. We are currently developing a new strategic plan in order to realize a 2020 vision for the museum. The fall of 2014 and early 2015 will be devoted to developing, and refining that plan, the final version of which will be implemented on July 1, 2015.

While evaluating the past four years, and beginning to plan for the next five, there are many lessons we have learned. We are now incorporating such feedback into this planning cycle. The most important results of this kind of process include:

1. Activities across the museum that are much more focused and cohesive (everyone has a better understanding of precisely *what* they are supposed to be doing).
2. A feeling among stakeholders that there is a lot of energy and activity, that the museum is livelier and more connected to the community.
3. A more active and connected board and donor community.
4. A new emphasis on people (i.e., our staff and volunteers) being our best asset—and a better understanding of how to develop and leverage their ideas and energy.
5. By keeping the focus on the bigger picture you can avoid short-term thinking that keeps you stuck "in the weeds" of the daily crises.

One of the most important next steps involves focusing on embedding innovative thinking throughout the organization. One of the primary components in the new strategic plan is to develop a broad view of succession planning—this includes a renewed focus on developing junior staff from within the organization, recruiting the right people into the right positions, as well as planning for inevitable changes at the highest levels of management and throughout the organization. Without understanding that situations change, people move on, and what works now will not always be the best way to handle things, we cannot sustain the organizational changes we have fought so hard to gain.

Innovation is so often seen as finding a new product or developing a wholly new program. While the TMA is certainly interested in those things as well, we have approached innovation differently. We have recognized that the way museums have traditionally been structured no longer fit the way the world now works, that those traditional structures could not take advantage of advances in technology and systems thinking to do jobs better and more efficiently, and that it was past time to innovate from within and to examine closely held beliefs about each role within the museum.

Ultimately, our job as museum leaders is to understand that the museum is larger than our time in it. When we inevitably move on (be that the next year or the next decade), we should know that the organization is stronger than when we arrived, better able to handle the current environment, and able to sustain itself and be relevant to its visitors and community in perpetuity.

KEY RESOURCES

Ancona, Deborah, Thomas W. Malone, Wanda J. Orlikowski, and Peter M. Senge. "In Praise of the Incomplete Leader." *Harvard Business Review*, February 2007.

Bryant, Adam. *The Corner Office: Indispensable and Unexpected Lessons from CEOs on How to Lead and Succeed*. St. Martin's Griffin; Reprint edition, 2012.

Center for Creative Leadership. *Developing a Leadership Strategy: A Critical Ingredient for Organizational Success*. Global Organizational Leadership Development, White Paper Series May, 2009.

HBR's 10 Must Reads on Change Management. Harvard Business Review Press; 1 edition 2011.

Hill, Linda A., Kent Lineback. *Being the Boss*, Harvard Business Review Press, 2011.

Innovatrium. http://www.innovatrium.org/.

Kotter, John. *Leading Change*, Harvard Business Review Press; 1 edition, 2012.

Predictive Index: http://www.piworldwide.com/solutions/predictive-index-system/.

NOTES

1. The ten questions asked of every group were: What were your best and fondest memories of the TMA? What have you been involved with personally at the TMA that gave you the greatest satisfaction? What is your burning issue in the community right now? Who are the people who could consume our product but do not? And how do we attract them? In five year's time what would you want to be different/the same about the TMA? What organizations, whether in Toledo or elsewhere, should we partner with to achieve our objectives? What exhibition projects should we undertake, with whom, and why? In what ways can we better leverage the expertise of our staff within the community? What should we do to make better use of the Peristyle (a large performance space)?

2. This article does not address the museum's extensive efforts around a different kind of sustainability—the reduction in energy use. Here, efforts over the past twenty years has resulted in an 80 percent reduction in energy costs. This savings is, in essence, a way of achieving a growth in an institution's operating budget devoted to programming without actually having to grow the budget.

Index

About the Contributors

Karen Coutts is an independent consultant and is the former director of development for the New Children's Museum. She has been an active part of the nonprofit sector for nearly twenty years, working with emerging and well-established nonprofit organizations. With a master's degree in art history from Boston University and significant expertise in infrastructure development, fundraising, and project management, she has positively impacted museums and arts organizations on both coasts.

Juilee Decker is an associate professor of museum studies at Rochester Institute of Technology. She earned her PhD from Case Western Reserve University. Decker's research interests and curation include public art, commemoration, and memory as well as the social application of museum informatics. Since 2008, she has served as editor of *Collections: A Journal for Museum and Archives Professionals*, a peer-reviewed journal published by Rowman & Littlefield.

Mike Deetsch is the assistant director of education at the Toledo Museum of Art. Prior to joining the Toledo Museum of Art in 2013, he served as student programs manager at the Kentucky Historical Society. He has over ten years of museum experience, programming for school age and family audiences in large metropolitan centers and small towns, as well as history and art museums.

Nancy Enterline, CFRE, is the vice president of membership and development at the Monterey Bay Aquarium. She holds a BA from Wake Forest University, a MS from Florida State University, and has worked in nonprofit communications and resource development for fifteen years.

Karen Gillenwater is a curator and museum educator with sixteen years professional experience in museums in the Louisville, Kentucky, area and Denver, Colorado, and seven years experience working with public art. After serving as curator at the Carnegie Center for Art & History for seven years, she assumed the post of museum manager at 21c Museum Hotel in Louisville. Gillenwater holds a master of arts in art history with a concentration in museums studies and a bachelor of arts in art history with a minor in business administration.

Amy Gilman is currently the associate director at the Toledo Museum of Art where she has been since 2005, first as the associate curator of modern and contemporary art, then as assistant director of collections for exhibitions. Previously Gilman worked at the Museum of Contemporary Art Cleveland and at the Museum of Contemporary Photography in Chicago.

Carl G. Hamm has twenty-five years of experience in the nonprofit sector in development, marketing, and executive positions. Recognized as a Certified Fund Raising Executive since 1998, he has worked in healthcare and with organizations representing practically every discipline of the arts, from public radio and chamber music to theater, ballet, and the visual arts.

Gregory Hardison is the participatory arts and programs administrator at the Kentucky Historical Society in Frankfort, Kentucky. He is dedicated to improving the lives of children and families in his community and serves as a board member of several related organizations.

Jill Hartz is director of the Jordan Schnitzer Museum of Art and serves as president of the Association of Academic Museums and Galleries (AAMG).

Peter J. Kim is the executive director of the Museum of Food and Drink, a nonprofit that is launching a first-of-its-kind food museum that explores the culture, history, science, production, and commerce of food and drink—with exhibits you can eat. Originally from the cornfields of central Illinois, Peter has been fortunate to have the opportunity to work around the world as a hunger policy advocate, a public health educator, a founder of an arts education nonprofit in Cameroon, and an international litigator.

Vicky U. Lee has raised over $40 million since joining Friends of the High Line in 2011 as director of the Campaign for the High Line. She earned an MA at the Centre for New Writing at the University of Manchester in 2007 and a BA with Honors in French and international relations (Latin America) from New York University. Lee speaks five languages and lives in Manhattan.

James G. Leventhal is director of development at San Francisco's Exploratorium. Prior to assuming this post in 2014, James served for four years as deputy director for development at the Contemporary Jewish Museum of San Francisco, where he was part of a leadership team that oversaw significant growth and stabilization following the opening of the museum's new signature facility. Leventhal has more than twenty-five years of experience in the arts and cultural sector.

Melissa A. Russo has more than twenty-three years experience in non-profit executive management, fundraising and board governance. She is currently the director of institutional advancement at Chabot Space & Science Center and was previously the executive director of the Western Museums Association.

Irina Zeylikovich serves as the foundation and government relations manager at the Bay Area Discovery Museum, having begun her career in museums a decade ago as an Exploratorium Explainer, and transitioning public programs expertise toward institutional development. She completed her undergraduate and graduate work at the University of California, Berkeley and the University of Michigan, respectively.